The Fu[illegible] Knowle[illegible]agement

Harnessing Artificial Intelligence

EDITED BY FRANCESCA RAMADAN

Commissioning editor
Francesca Ramadan

Managing director
Sian O'Neill

The Future of Legal Knowledge Management: Harnessing Artificial Intelligence
is published by

Globe Law and Business Ltd
3 Mylor Close
Horsell
Woking
Surrey GU21 4DD
United Kingdom
Tel: +44 20 3745 4770
www.globelawandbusiness.com

The Future of Legal Knowledge Management: Harnessing Artificial Intelligence

ISBN 978-1-83723-167-6
EPUB ISBN 978-1-83723-168-3
Adobe PDF ISBN 978-1-83723-169-0

GPSR Compliance: EU Authorised Representative: Easy Access System Europe - Mustamäe tee 50, 10621 Tallinn, Estonia, gpsr.requests@easproject.com

Contents

Executive summary

Legal knowledge management (KM) used to mean vast law firm libraries, filing cabinets stocked with briefs, and decades of professional experience and institutional knowledge locked in senior partners' minds. As digital transformation swept through the legal industry, these evolved into document management systems and searchable databases. Although these tools represented a significant improvement, fundamental limitations remained in their ability to extract meaning from data and make connections across different sources of information. As artificial intelligence (AI) becomes increasingly embedded in law firm operations, KM professionals and teams find their role evolving, moving beyond pure practice support into a more strategic function that directly impacts firm profitability, operational efficiency, and competitive differentiation. KM professionals will play a critical role moving forward in the era of AI.

However, this shift can only be achieved when KM practitioners are equipped with the right tools, skills, and resources. *The Future of Legal Knowledge Management: Harnessing Artificial Intelligence* provides innovative and robust solutions to some of the most pressing issues facing KM practitioners today. Within the following pages, readers will explore the ways in which knowledge managers can build a strong data foundation for AI application; how to develop the AI-empowered lawyer; gaining organizational and partner support for AI-augmented legal KM; modernizing existing KM architecture in the age of AI; and navigating the implementation of agentic AI. Written by KM experts, technologists, and industry leaders, *The Future of Legal Knowledge Management: Harnessing Artificial Intelligence* serves as a comprehensive handbook for KM professionals seeking to develop their skills, broaden their expertise, and overcome the challenges presented by modern legal practice. It will equip readers with the data-driven insights and actionable strategies needed to navigate a rapidly evolving profession, embrace AI's potential, and harness its power to shape the future of KM.

We begin with an exploration of decision intelligence – guided by Dr

Andrea Miskolczi, managing director of InterAlia Consulting – as a practical framework for understanding KM's strategic importance in law firms. Chapter 1 outlines how legal decisions rely on the interaction of data and KM, AI, domain expertise, and human judgment, and provides an overview of why many law firms have struggled to use their knowledge effectively. As elaborated within this chapter, decision intelligence can assist firms in overcoming these challenges by clarifying the value of curated, structured, and contextualized information. Particular emphasis is placed on data and KM, which form the essential foundation for reliable decisions and responsible adoption of AI. The chapter also highlights the parallels between legal knowledge managers and data analysts in other sectors, demonstrating that legal work requires similar capabilities for data quality, structure, and context. By framing knowledge as a decision asset, Andrea makes the case for decision intelligence as a means of strengthening the strategic role of KM and providing a new framework for integrating AI into legal practice.

Generative AI has burst into the legal scene in the last few years and is the hottest topic of discussion amongst legal tech professionals. Many law firms have made significant investments in AI-driven products, and there is a growing sense that AI is going to be transformative in relation to the delivery of KM services, as well as to the broader provision of legal services to clients. However, many firms are still struggling to harness this technology effectively. Some have yet to realize significant returns from their investments, and many have found that adoption levels are disappointing. Others are struggling to know where to start in applying the technology within their practice, and persistent concerns about hallucination risks – magnified by some well-publicized courtroom blunders – are further hampering progress in many organizations. In Chapter 2, Mark Ford, knowledge, data, and AI strategy consultant, offers a practical guide on how to analyze legal tasks in order to identify the areas in which AI could provide support. This chapter provides examples of KM activities, as well as broader legal work, that can be supported and streamlined by the thoughtful application of AI, and offers tips and guidance on how to mitigate the risk of hallucinations and other errors.

Building on this practical foundation, in Chapter 3, co-authors Grant Newton – lead consultant at Atlas by ClearPeople – and Sarah Pullin – global director of knowledge at Baker McKenzie – take a deep dive into why exactly data quality and integrity is so fundamental to enabling the effective, safe, and successful application of AI for legal KM, with an emphasis on the fact that the reliability of AI outcomes is directly shaped by the type, accuracy, completeness, and contextual depth of the input. Data, therefore, must be treated as a strategic asset, with proper governance and taxonomy alignment necessary to guarantee understanding and reliability. Grant and Sarah offer practical advice to assist with ensuring data quality, such as quality definitions based on type and purpose and consistent tagging, grading, reviews, and retention and archiving processes. Aligned to the mechanics of managing data, the chapter also discusses the continued involvement of people in the process, focusing on adoption, training, collaboration, and change management to build accountability and adaptability. Chapter 3 concludes by raising awareness of risk management and compliance considerations, highlighting pressing ethical, legal, regulatory, and security challenges and the need for adaptable strategies that sustain trust and responsibility as AI continues to reshape the way people work.

Continuing the book's practical exploration of how AI can elevate legal knowledge work, Chapter 4 – authored by Mark Gediman, senior research analyst at Alston & Bird LLP, and Kevin Miles, library manager at Norton Rose Fulbright US LLP – focuses on making AI "work for you from the inside out" by unlocking the value of firms' internal data and systems. The authors begin with a familiar challenge: research requests that require navigating disparate document management systems, contract relationship management systems, and financial databases, where traditional search tools often return overwhelming, decontextualized results. They demonstrate how generative AI – in particular, accessible tools like Microsoft Copilot – can unify these internal repositories, reduce noise, and reveal context-rich insights that previously required hours of manual cross-referencing. Mark and Kevin emphasize the practical realities of implementation, underscoring the need for secure deployment, prevention of data leakage, and user training to ensure AI outputs are treated as informed starting points, rather than authoritative answers. They further illustrate these principles through detailed examples, such as generating experience profiles, competitive intelligence templates, state law surveys, trend analyses, and SWOT reports. The chapter concludes by positioning AI as a long-awaited step change in enterprise search: a tool that can finally make decades of firm knowledge quickly accessible, provided that users verify results, understand limitations, and pair AI capabilities with human judgment.

When discussing the transformative impact of AI on legal work and KM practice, we would be remiss to overlook the rise of the AI agent. Chapter 5, authored by Chad Ergun, chief information officer at Womble Bond Dickinson, explores one of the most consequential developments in legal AI: the emergence of agentic systems. Unlike traditional AI tools that execute discrete tasks, agentic AI retains context, pursues goals through multi-step reasoning, and improves through feedback captured in persistent memory. As these systems shift from experimentation to everyday legal practice, Chad argues that firms must rethink how humans and machines collaborate. This evolution redefines the role of KM professionals, who move beyond curating tools to becoming workflow architects and AI-behavior designers, skilled in prompt chaining, context engineering, and structured training loops. This is illustrated through practical examples of applications such as continuous matter lifecycle analysis, automated knowledge extraction, and building expertise networks powered by shared agentic memory. One particularly powerful use case is the creation of "mentor agents" that capture and model the work patterns of senior partners. With proper governance and consent, these persona-based agents can analyze negotiation styles, redlines, and commentary to provide on-demand guidance to associates, preserving decades of institutional wisdom long after partners retire. Ultimately, this chapter emphasizes that the success of agentic AI rests on human competencies – understanding intent, constraints, and context – rather than technical prompting alone. By designing grounded, auditable, and aligned agents, KM teams can transform static knowledge into adaptive systems that extend human judgment and deliver consistently reliable outcomes.

Our discussion of the human element continues in Chapter 6, authored by Hélène Russell, knowledge and learning specialist at TheKnowledgeBusiness. Hélène argues that KM professionals must be the ones to lead law firms through the cultural and operational shifts required to successfully integrate AI – particularly generative and agentic AI – into legal practice. As this chapter explains, lawyers' well-documented preferences for autonomy, perfectionism, and certainty create predictable resistance to imperfect or evolving AI tools, making structured change management essential. Drawing on decades of behavioral research, this chapter introduces a suite of practical frameworks to guide KM-led adoption efforts, including Rogers' Diffusion model for understanding adopter groups; Rock's SCARF to reduce threat responses; Lewin and Kotter's models for structured transformation; and the Heath brothers' Switch approach for motivating lasting behavioral change. This chapter also highlights how nudge theory, self-determination theory, and purpose-alignment thinking can be used to design AI-enabled workflows that feel intuitive, fair, and meaningful to practitioners. The importance of communication in the implementation of AI initiatives is reinforced: to ensure success, KM professionals are urged to apply customer journey principles, tailor messages to distinct audiences, and reinforce key themes through repeated, transparent updates. Ultimately, Hélène contends that AI adoption is not a technology problem, but a people problem. KM professionals – with their deep expertise in governance, communication, and cultural change – are uniquely positioned to move firms from resistance to sustainable, firm-wide AI-augmented practice.

Sustainability is also the central theme of Chapter 7, authored by Katya Linossi – co-founder and CEO of Atlas by ClearPeople – who examines the escalating urgency for law firms to capture, structure, and scale their expertise in an era defined by hybrid work, rising client expectations, and the ubiquity of AI. She emphasizes that, while AI tools promise unprecedented productivity, their effectiveness depends on rich, validated, and contextual knowledge foundations. Much of a firm's intelligence – particularly tacit knowledge – remains locked in lawyers' heads or scattered across informal workspaces, making it inaccessible to both humans and machines. Unlocking this expertise is now mission-critical: it enables responsible AI use, strengthens decision-making, and ensures institutional wisdom is not lost through attrition or fragmented workflows. This chapter outlines practical strategies for scaling knowledge, from capturing informal insights in the flow of work to extracting tacit expertise through debriefs, mentoring, and emerging AI-enabled methods, such as dynamic expertise networks and digital twins. Katya also highlights the importance of democratizing access to knowledge through workflow-embedded tools, intelligent search, managed openness, and robust governance. Ultimately, she positions modern KM as the architect of a living, learning ecosystem that blends human judgment with machine intelligence. Firms that build such systems – where knowledge is continually captured, contextualized, shared, and reused – will convert expertise into sustainable competitive advantage in the AI-enabled future.

We conclude with an alternative perspective, provided by Dr Pietro Brambilla, senior counsel at Mercedes-Benz Group AG and legal innovation consultant at InterAlia Consulting, who shifts the lens in Chapter 8 to examine what sophisticated clients now expect from their law firms. Corporate legal departments have undergone a profound transformation: once slow-moving and document-bound, they now operate "at the speed of data," driven by real-time business demands that cannot wait for traditional legal timelines. Accelerated by generative AI, many in-house teams have vaulted beyond the maturity of law firms, adopting advanced data architectures that enable automated legal work, dynamic spend analysis, performance benchmarking, and predictive decision-making. From this outside-in vantage point, Pietro reveals a new hierarchy of client expectations: structured, machine-readable data that integrates seamlessly with enterprise systems; quantifiable indicators of expertise and value; and continuously updated intelligence that feeds clients' internal analytics. Rather than viewing these expectations as disruptive, this chapter positions them as a strategic catalyst for KM leaders. Client demand provides the clearest mandate yet for firms to modernize and embrace secure cloud platforms, robust APIs, and unified knowledge and data infrastructures. In this landscape, firms whose KM teams lead the redesign of systems to meet client data needs will elevate their strategic relevance and compete on insight and value, while those that lag risk being reduced to price-driven providers.

About the authors

Dr Pietro Brambilla, LL.M., brings a rare combination of legal expertise and technical leadership to the intersection of law, data and AI. As former head of digital transformation for integrity and legal affairs at Mercedes-Benz, he pioneered groundbreaking initiatives in legal operations, implementing agile methodologies, data-driven knowledge management, and AI-augmented workflows across a global legal department.

Pietro also has served as data officer and information security officer for legal and compliance, architecting the data infrastructure that enables AI-driven decision-making. His hands-on experience in leveraging and deploying AI systems provides unique insight into both the technical requirements and organizational change management needed for successful transformation.

Now back in a more traditional legal in-house role at Mercedes-Benz, Pietro also serves as a consultant with InterAlia, a boutique legal innovation consultancy. Through this work, he shares his expertise in AI strategy, data architecture, and digital transformation with law firms and legal departments across Europe, helping organizations turn innovation initiatives into lasting impact.

Chad Ergun is a visionary technology leader who currently serves as chief information officer at Womble Bond Dickinson, one of the largest AmLaw100 law firms in the United States, with 1,300 attorneys across 37 offices. With over 25 years of experience in the technology sector, Ergun has established himself as a pioneering force in legal technology innovation, specializing in the integration of cutting-edge technologies like generative AI, machine learning, and advanced data analytics into law firm operations.

Chad focuses on driving AI transformation and process automation into reliable systems that lawyers can adopt naturally. His areas of expertise include generative AI, knowledge management, cybersecurity, eDiscovery, machine learning, and data science.

A frequent contributor to the legal technology community, Chad has co-authored publications, hosted podcasts, and presented at international forums on the intersection of law and emerging technology. He is a visible advocate for responsible AI that improves client service, strengthens security, and frees lawyers to focus on high-value work.

Mark Ford is a legal knowledge management and innovation leader with nearly three decades of experience in transforming how global law firms deliver legal services. A pioneer in legal innovation since the early 2000s, he has worked at the intersection of law and technology since the emergence of modern legal tech, driving large-scale change across people, processes, and platforms. He has held senior roles at Clifford Chance, Baker McKenzie, and EY Law, where he led global KM, operations, and technology-enabled transformation initiatives. As an independent consultant, he advises leading firms on AI strategy, enterprise data and knowledge architecture, organizational design, change management, and the implementation and adoption of technology tools and platforms.

Mark Gediman is a senior research analyst for Alston & Bird LLP. He is past president of the Southern California Association of Law Libraries (SCALL), as well as co-founder and co-chair of the PLLIP-SIS Competitive Intelligence Caucus. Mark writes and presents regularly on competitive intelligence, research, and library management issues for the American Association of Law Libraries (AALL), the California Lawyers Association, the Legal Marketing Association (LMA), the Special Libraries Association (SLA), the Southwestern Association of Law Libraries (SWALL), SCALL, the Northern California Association of Law Libraries (NOCALL), ACI, and Houston Area Law Librarians (HALL). He contributed to several books, including *Business Intelligence for Law Firms* (Ark Group, 2012), *Innovations in Legal KM* (Ark Group, 2017), *Strategic Intelligence for Law Firms* (Ark Group, 2018), and *AI and The Legal Profession* (Globe Law & Business, 2025), and has had articles featured in several magazines and journals, including *AALL Spectrum*, *Practicing Law Management Week*, *Paralegal Today*, and *Facts & Findings*. Mark is a graduate of the University of California–Riverside.

Katya Linossi is a visionary leader who is redefining knowledge in the age of AI. As co-founder and CEO of ClearPeople, she guided the company from being featured on the prestigious eConsultancy 100 list to its transformation in 2019 with the creation of Atlas, an intelligent knowledge platform that helps law firms and professional services organizations connect people, knowledge, and technology in new ways.

Building on her MBA research into knowledge management in law firms, Katya has been deeply engaged with the legal and KM community for more than two decades. Through Atlas, she continues to work closely with leading law firms to advance how knowledge is shared, discovered, and applied.

Kevin Miles is the co-chair of the Competitive Intelligence Group of the American Association of Law Libraries with Mark Gediman. He works as the manager of research services in the Dallas office of Norton Rose Fulbright. Kevin is passionate about the application of AI to competitive intelligence.

Andrea Miskolczi helps legal leaders turn innovation ambition into operational reality. As managing director of InterAlia Consulting, she works with law firms and in-house legal teams facing stalled legaltech projects, low adoption rates, and fragmented innovation efforts. Her clients typically struggle to align their strategy with day-to-day execution, build internal buy-in, and deliver measurable outcomes.

Andrea began her career as a practicing lawyer at Clifford Chance and Linklaters before moving into leadership roles in innovation, business development, and marketing at Wolf Theiss and Dentons. She has led cross-border, award-winning initiatives that have been recognized by the *Financial Times'* Innovative Lawyers Program for their impact on collaboration, client experience, data literacy, and workflow automation. With experience spanning the UK, Germany, Austria, and Hungary, and leadership roles undertaken throughout Continental Europe and Central and Eastern Europe, Andrea brings a pragmatic, pan-European lens to what actually works – and what doesn't – when modernizing legal functions.

Grant Newton is an outcome-focused delivery professional with a track record of embedding enduring capabilities through new technologies and processes across a range of industries. At ClearPeople, he is responsible for ensuring the successful delivery of the Atlas knowledge platform and Atlas Fuse (AI capability). He achieves this by assessing options and designing solutions to meet the more complex requirements and using the full suite of Atlas components available, leveraging the M365 platform or ClearPeople's ecosystem of supported third-party integrated solutions.

Grant has worked in technology for over 30 years as a project manager, consultant, architect, and business analyst, with eight of those years spent working directly for law firms to deliver search, knowledge, document, extranet, intranet, and website solutions.

Sarah Pullin is the global director of knowledge at Baker McKenzie and part of the global leadership team. She leads knowledge lawyers, KM managers, information and research teams, global knowledge experts, four offshore knowledge teams, and KM systems and tools in support of the firm's clients and business strategy. Sarah qualified and practiced as a lawyer before becoming a professional support lawyer and has spent over 20 years managing and leading all aspects of knowledge, including now being a global lead on generative AI and digital upgrades.

Hélène Russell of TheKnowledgeBusiness is a specialist in knowledge management with 20 years' experience and a particular interest in knowledge sharing cultures, trust, and complexity. After working in clinical negligence litigation defense work for eight years and spending two years as a knowledge lawyer, Hélène completed an executive MBA, studying antecedents to knowledge sharing for her dissertation. She has now worked as a self-employed KM consultant since 2008.

Hélène is the chair of the CILIP Knowledge and Information Management Special Interest Group and a core committee member of the UK Knowledge Mobilisation Forum, delivering an annual highly interactive conference for health and social care sectors. She is a judge for both the CILIP K&IM awards and the LexisNexis KM awards.

Hélène has chaired and spoken at various international conferences, including BIALL, CILIP, KM Legal, Lexpo, Butterworth's PSL conference, and for UWE and St Andrew's University. She runs global online training and networking groups (Knowledge Network and the Next Gen Alliances) and offers KM training through MBL, Falconbury/IPI Academy, CILIP, and bespoke in-house training.

Hélène is the author of *Knowledge Management Handbook* (The Law Society, 2012) and *Practical Projects in Legal KM: A year of living knowledgeably* (Legal Monitor, 2015); a contributor to five books by Globe Law and Business; and the author of a regular column (KIM Matters) for *Information Professional*.

Chapter 1:
Why KM matters more than ever: a decision intelligence perspective

By Dr Andrea Miskolczi, MBA, managing director, InterAlia Consulting

Knowledge has always been at the center of the identity and performance of law firms. It influences the quality of legal advice; the efficiency of legal processes; and the consistency with which firms serve clients. However, despite its importance, knowledge management (KM) has not been consistently understood, invested in, or embedded across the profession. Only a handful of firms have achieved a sustained and structured approach to KM; many others continue to struggle with the same challenges they faced when KM first emerged as a formal discipline. These challenges include limited coordination, difficulty capturing tacit insight, inconsistent behaviors, unclear ownership, and a general uncertainty about the value that KM provides.

Artificial intelligence (AI) has amplified these challenges. On one hand, it has raised expectations about how quickly and efficiently legal work can be performed; on the other, it has revealed the consequences of neglecting KM. Large language models require structured, curated, and contextualized data in order to produce useful results. They depend on the same knowledge foundations that many firms have found difficult to establish. At the same time, lawyers encounter mixed messages about what AI can do. Some narratives suggest that AI will generate ready-to-use content simply by being placed on top of a document management system; others speculate about AI replacing lawyers entirely; and many narrow the conversation to chat interfaces, rather than examining the broader role of knowledge, judgment, and process design.

In this environment, the concept of decision intelligence (DI) provides clarity. DI is already used in other sectors as a means of understanding how decisions are made; what information feeds into them; and how data, technology, expertise, and human judgment interact. When applied to legal work, DI provides law firms with a way to understand the true value of their data, their documents, and their KM activities. It also offers a language for explaining how AI contributes to legal work and why human judgment remains essential.

This chapter explores how DI can help KM professionals articulate their role more clearly. It discusses why law firms have struggled to use their knowledge effectively; what DI brings to legal consulting and legal processes; and how the four components of DI interact in legal work. Particular emphasis is placed on the first component, which concerns data and KM. This focus reflects the central role that knowledge professionals play in shaping the foundations on which AI and human expertise rely.

Why law firms struggle to use their knowledge

KM as a low organizational priority

Despite frequent recognition of its importance, KM has rarely been treated as a sustained organizational priority. Competing pressures, billable hour demands, and limited resources have often reduced KM to a series of initiatives that are difficult to maintain over time. In many firms, KM has been viewed as a support activity, rather than as a driver of legal quality or operational performance. Because the value of knowledge work has not always been clear, investment has been inconsistent: some firms invested heavily in technology but very little in the people needed to curate and manage knowledge; others invested in specialist roles, but did not build the processes and governance required for sustained impact. The result of these inconsistent approaches has been a landscape in which many firms have incomplete knowledge resources, outdated precedents, and repositories that reflect document storage, rather than organizational learning. These gaps have significant implications in the context of AI, which depends on structured and reliable data.

The complexity of legal data

Law firms generate vast amounts of data. This includes contracts, drafts, mark-ups, email threads, research notes, legal opinions, negotiation histories, and client guidance. Much of this content sits in multiple systems and lacks consistent metadata. The same clause might appear in dozens of versions, and the same template might exist in multiple practice groups with minor variations. Without curation and structure, this volume becomes noise, rather than insight. Lawyers may struggle to find examples that are accurate, relevant, and suitable for reuse. AI systems face the same challenge: they can process large datasets, but they require clear indicators of quality and context in order to produce meaningful results.

Tacit knowledge and the limits of documentation

Legal practice relies heavily on tacit knowledge. Lawyers draw on experience, intuition, and subtle understanding of how clients operate; they assess commercial risk, read negotiation dynamics, and interpret ambiguous information. Much of this knowledge is not written down; in many cases, it is difficult to articulate explicitly. KM has long struggled with the challenge of capturing these insights in ways that others can use. Without processes such as debriefs, knowledge interviews, or structured capture, valuable insights remain siloed.

Behavioral challenges

KM depends on behavior. Lawyers must contribute knowledge, use the resources provided, and engage with tools and processes. These behaviors are shaped by incentives, habits, cultural expectations, and workload pressures. When the value of KM is unclear, engagement drops. When engagement is inconsistent, content quality declines. These dynamics create a cycle that is difficult to break.

The impact of AI on knowledge expectations

AI has intensified the need for clarity. Many lawyers expect AI tools to work immediately and flawlessly, even when the underlying knowledge base is inconsistent or incomplete. Others fear that AI will diminish the importance of expertise or replace the work lawyers do. Both views oversimplify how AI functions and fail to acknowledge the importance of structured, curated, and contextualized knowledge. DI provides a framework for addressing these misunderstandings.

What DI brings to legal work

DI clarifies how decisions are made and how different components contribute to the outcome. Although originally developed in data-intensive industries, its principles align closely with the realities of legal consulting and legal processes. DI encourages firms to identify the decisions lawyers make during a matter, the information required to support those decisions, and the judgment needed to interpret that information in context.

Focusing on decisions in legal consulting and processes

Law firms make many business decisions, but this chapter focuses specifically on decisions related to legal matters. These include choices about drafting, negotiation, risk, strategy, and client guidance. DI offers a structured way to analyze these decisions – it shows which decisions depend on curated documents, which rely on domain expertise, and which can be supported by AI.

Bringing structure and transparency to decisions

DI separates decisions into components. These include the information inputs; the assumptions that shape interpretation; the constraints that apply; and the criteria used to evaluate options. By making these elements explicit, DI increases transparency and consistency. It also shows where KM contributes and where human judgment plays an essential role.

Demystifying AI

DI clarifies that AI operates within boundaries. It can support classification, extraction, pattern recognition, and text generation. However, its performance depends on the quality of inputs and the clarity of the decision context. DI helps lawyers understand that AI is not a source of truth; instead, it is a tool that requires strong data foundations and human oversight.

The four components of DI

DI identifies four components that shape decisions in legal work. These components provide a structured way to understand how data, KM, AI, domain expertise, and human judgment interact.

1. Data and KM

Data and KM provide the foundation for decision-making. Legal decisions rely on documents, templates, examples, research, and contextual insights. For these materials to support decisions effectively, they must be accurate, curated, anonymized, and accessible. Knowledge managers structure this information, maintain quality, and ensure that lawyers can rely on it.

2. AI

AI can process large datasets, identify patterns, automate classification, and generate suggestions. It can support many aspects of legal work. However, AI is only as good as the data it receives. Without strong knowledge foundations, AI systems will produce inconsistent results.

3. Domain knowledge

Domain knowledge is the legal expertise and practical experience that informs interpretation. Lawyers draw on doctrine, precedent, market norms, and client expectations. Domain knowledge shapes how information is understood and how decisions are made.

4. Human judgment

Human judgment incorporates behavioral and contextual factors. It includes risk assessment, negotiation strategy, client advisory skills, and professional intuition. DI acknowledges that human judgment cannot be automated; instead, it demonstrates the ways in which data and technology can support judgment.

Figure 1: The four components of decision intelligence

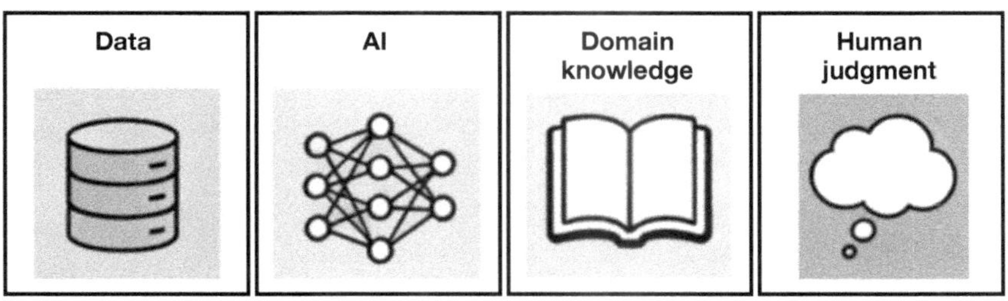

The central role of data and KM

Although all four components are important, the first component is particularly relevant for KM professionals. The performance of AI and the effectiveness of decisions depend on the quality of the data that knowledge managers curate, enrich, and maintain.

Learning from other industries

Other industries recognized the importance of data long before AI became mainstream. Banks, insurers, retailers, and technology companies hired large numbers of data analysts and data scientists. These professionals clean, structure, label, anonymize, and interpret data. They provide the foundation on which sophisticated models depend.

If we describe what a legal data analyst would do, the connection to KM is immediate. A legal data analyst would identify high-quality documents, remove sensitive information, label content with metadata, organize clause libraries, record negotiation outcomes, and maintain structured datasets.

These tasks overlap significantly with the traditional work of knowledge managers.

The difference is that other industries view these tasks as essential to decision-making, and invest accordingly. Law firms have the same needs, but their investment in knowledge roles has been limited by unclear expectations and inconsistent prioritization. DI helps bridge this gap by demonstrating that KM is the legal profession's equivalent to data management in other sectors.

Curating legal data

Knowledge managers assess quality, remove outdated content, and validate best practice examples. Without this curation, lawyers and AI systems will rely on inconsistent or unsuitable materials. Curation becomes especially important when document repositories include drafts, negotiated exceptions, or non-standard language.

Structuring content for use

Metadata, categorization, and taxonomies make content findable and usable. AI tools amplify the impact of good structure, because they rely on patterns and semantic relationships. Knowledge managers design these structures, apply them to content, and maintain them over time.

Capturing context

Context distinguishes a good document from a merely relevant one. Knowledge managers capture insights about why decisions were made, what trade-offs were accepted, and how client priorities influenced outcomes. This context helps lawyers interpret documents and helps AI systems learn from meaningful examples.

Enabling safe and effective AI adoption

Knowledge managers provide the governance required for responsible use of AI. They understand where AI can assist and where it requires oversight and ensure that models draw on reliable data and that outputs are validated. DI supports this governance by clarifying the boundaries of automation.

Interactions between the four components

Data and KM as the base layer

Without structured, curated, and contextualized knowledge, the other components falter. AI cannot classify or generate content effectively; domain expertise cannot be shared efficiently; and human judgment is not supported by reliable information.

AI as a dependent component

AI amplifies the value of well-managed knowledge, but exposes weaknesses in unstructured repositories. DI shows where AI performs well and where it requires human oversight.

Domain knowledge as the interpretive component

Domain knowledge provides the lens through which information is understood. Knowledge managers support domain expertise by providing structured examples, guidance notes, and curated content.

Human judgment as the integrative component

Human judgment brings together information, analysis, experience, and behavioral insight. DI acknowledges the central role of human judgment and avoids narratives that suggest automation will replace lawyers entirely.

Practical implications for KM professionals

KM professionals can use DI to strengthen their role in several ways.

Define knowledge tasks through decision-making needs

DI clarifies which decisions require which types of knowledge. Knowledge managers can identify the documents, metadata, and insights needed for each decision and design processes accordingly.

Align knowledge structures with legal processes

Knowledge managers can structure content to reflect decision points in legal processes. This includes categorizing clauses by risk level, structuring templates around decision pathways, and aligning guidance with workflow stages.

Develop legal data management skills

Knowledge managers can adopt techniques used by data analysts, such as data cleaning, labelling, quality control, and pattern recognition. These skills strengthen the data foundations required for AI.

Provide governance for AI

Knowledge managers can lead the development of standards for training data, reviewing outputs, and integrating AI tools into workflows.

Strengthen collaboration with lawyers

DI provides a shared language that helps lawyers to understand the value of KM. Knowledge managers can explain how curated content, context, and structured data support decision-making and improve legal outcomes.

Conclusions

DI offers a practical and structured way to understand how data, KM, AI, domain knowledge, and human judgment interact in legal work. It helps law firms move beyond simplistic narratives about AI and toward a more grounded understanding of how legal decisions are made. It also elevates the role of KM by showing that curated, structured, and contextualized knowledge is the foundation on which AI and human expertise rely.

For KM professionals, DI provides an opportunity to articulate their value more clearly, strengthen their partnership with lawyers, and shape the conditions for responsible and effective use of AI in legal practice. By adopting this framework, firms can build environments in which decisions are informed, consistent, and supported by the best available knowledge.

Chapter 2:

What AI can do for you: a KM practitioner's guide

By Mark Ford, knowledge, data, and AI strategy consultant

The arrival of ChatGPT in November 2022 took the world by storm, as users quickly began to see the potential impact of this new generative AI (genAI) technology. Its extraordinary capabilities and even greater potential were quickly and widely acknowledged, with ChatGPT reaching 100 million users in the space of two months. As a comparison, the internet took seven years, with mobile phones taking more than 16 years, to reach the same milestone.

Initial uses were mostly for personal or domestic purposes; although it soon became clear that there were also wide potential applications of genAI in the business world, law firms and other professional services organizations have been slower to adopt the technology. This is partly due to the cautious nature of the legal profession: any new tool, process, or technology must be carefully tested and evaluated before it will be accepted for use in legal practice. A number of high-profile disasters, in which lawyers presented non-existent precedents that were the products of so-called "hallucinations" by a genAI tool in court, have also played a part by highlighting the potential risks to many practitioners. In *Mata v. Avianca, Inc*, for example, the plaintiff's lawyers cited a number of cases that the judge later described as "bogus judicial decisions, with bogus quotes and bogus internal citations."

Additionally, in the UK High Court case of *Hamad Al-Haroun v. Qatar National Bank*, many of the authorities cited by the claimant turned out to be fictions generated by a publicly available genAI tool.

Furthermore, some early adopters experimented with the first generation of tools and found much of their output unreliable, especially when it came to tasks that required an understanding of legal concepts. There may be a few reasons for this. First, it is true that some tasks are more suitable than others for genAI tools, and this chapter will explore that in further detail. In addition, however, it is undeniable that the sophistication of the available tools has increased significantly since the first release of ChatGPT, and there are now many products on the market that use a large language model (LLM) that has been specifically trained on legal content. Sceptics should consider the blistering pace of change in this field and the exponential increase in the capabilities of available tools before dismissing the technology on the basis of prior shortcomings.

A further significant barrier to adoption, however, remains a lack of understanding as to how best to harness genAI. Many KM professionals perceive that they *should* be using the technology – both in their own work and in supporting their lawyer stakeholders – but they are unsure where to start and concerned about the potential risks. This chapter offers a framework for analyzing which areas of KM and legal practice lend themselves to the application of genAI technology; sets out practical steps that individuals can take to get started on their genAI journey or to make further progress along the road; and provides practical examples of tasks that could partly or wholly be delegated to a genAI tool.

Where to start

Experiment with the available tools

As a starting point, it's important to familiarize yourself with the capabilities of genAI tools. If you have never tried or have limited experience of using tools like ChatGPT, Claude, Gemini, Llama, and others, a good starting point would be to experiment with them. The majority are available for free; in most cases, you can unlock more powerful features for about the same monthly price as a Netflix subscription.

Many users start by using a genAI tool in their private life – this is a perfectly good way to start to gain familiarity with them. Need help writing a covering letter for a job application? Claude will bring out the key points of your experience if you point it at your LinkedIn profile and upload your CV. Going to a new city and need ideas for what to do? Gemini will put together a day's itinerary for you, taking your particular interests and preferences into account. Dealing with a troublesome error on your home laptop? ChatGPT will help you to resolve it quickly. (The last example is one of which this author has significant personal experience!)

These examples are not business-related, but experiments like these will teach novices what the platforms do well and where their limits are. It will also teach users to craft good prompts, which is an important skill in getting the best out of genAI tools. Broadly speaking, the more background and context you provide, and the more specific you are about the output you are looking for, the better your result will be. Users who craft lazy prompts rarely get responses that precisely fit their needs.

As you experiment more with genAI tools in your personal life, you will naturally begin to see the potential applications of the technology to your professional life. The experience you have gained will give you the confidence and know-how to ensure that you are using the tools appropriately and getting the results that you expect.

Some users may be initially concerned about the possibility of errors or hallucinations in the output of genAI. In many circumstances, AI output can be more consistent and reliable than the output of a human; in any event, most responses can be checked and verified before any action is taken. More experienced users will also find ways to mitigate the risk of errors and hallucinations by crafting careful prompts. In any event, a zero-error rate is not essential for many tasks, so this need not be a determining factor in selecting where and when to use genAI. In most instances, the better test is whether the technology will save users time overall or help to produce a better result than would otherwise be possible.

Get your data in order

Once you start to gain more experience of using the tools, it will become clear that the quality of the output is, in large part, determined by the quality of the input. This partly means crafting thoughtful and detailed prompts, but equally important is the underlying repository on which the AI tool is basing its answers. For legally-trained LLMs, the platform will already have a good deal of legal-specific know-how to draw on, but most organizations will also wish to add their own knowledge repository into the mix.

This highlights the importance of ensuring that your organization's data is in good order. When genAI first appeared on the scene, many individuals and firms thought that this signaled the end of the need for data architecture, content curation, and even search tools – the AI would be able to do it all. However, it has quickly become clear that, while genAI tools can perform many of these tasks, they will not produce good results without a foundation of good-quality underlying data. Consider a drafting task, for example: a genAI tool can create a draft legal document with ease, but it will only produce a good document if it has good material to work with. It cannot produce content from thin air. The old adage – attributed to George Fuechsel – of "garbage in, garbage out" is equally true of the application of genAI: in fact, if you apply a genAI tool to a low-quality data set, you are in effect turbo-charging your garbage!

The classification of material, including the use of taxonomies, is another area where genAI has a part to play; however, it is also the case that even the best AI tool cannot create meaningful structure out of nowhere. If you ask it to classify documents without providing any structure to its output, no genAI tool will produce results at usable levels of quality and consistency. Ensuring that your data are thoughtfully structured, therefore, is more important than ever.

A new and undoubtedly true axiom of "IA before AI" (meaning that firms should put in place a robust information architecture before applying AI to their data) is fast entering the legal technology lexicon. Curating content to ensure that good-quality material is available to the AI and putting a robust data architecture in place to provide the AI a framework within which to work are both critical elements to success in any genAI project.

A model for analyzing knowledge management and legal tasks

One of the most potentially daunting tasks is to figure out which areas of your daily work will lend themselves best to the application of genAI. The following model may be useful in considering this. At a very high level, almost everything that legal professionals do breaks down into one of three categories: read, think, and write. Knowledge management (KM) practitioners read a new case, a legal document that has been submitted as knowhow, or a subscription agreement for a legal news product; they consider the impact of the new case, evaluate the quality of the document as a knowledge product, or assess the benefits and risks of the subscription agreement; and they then create some educational content about the new case, draft an abstract of the document, or mark up the draft subscription agreement.

Similarly, practicing lawyers read a contract, a new law, or a court document; they then consider the implications, the strengths and weaknesses of their argument, or the best advice to offer their client; and, finally, they create a revised draft of the contract, a written piece of advice, or a submission to the court in response.

While this model is, of course, an oversimplification of the complex nature of legal work, it can be helpful in considering where and how to apply genAI in practice.

Read

The "read" element of legal work – whether carried out by a KM practitioner or a practicing lawyer – is often thought of as the task that can most readily be delegated to AI. Indeed, the legal industry has been using a form of AI – machine learning – on large-scale document review exercises, such as electronic discovery and due diligence reviews for some years. The business case for using AI to review large numbers of documents to look for those relevant to a particular legal issue, or to identify those containing a particular provision, is well-established. However, the potential scope of review-based tasks that genAI can carry out on behalf of KM practitioners and lawyers is by no means limited to high-volume review exercises. Even when reviewing single documents or a small number of documents, AI will almost always outperform a human reviewer in terms of speed. The capabilities of AI technology in relation to the review of documents are discussed further below.

Think

This element of legal work is often less intuitively obvious as an area in which AI technology can be readily applied. While it is still true – for the time being, at least – that there are thought-based legal tasks that cannot be undertaken by AI, that does not mean that AI has no role to play in this space. Indeed, there are at least two major ways in which AI can add value here.

First, genAI is, by its nature, a generator of ideas. It can be very useful to think of it as a tool to use to come up with a rough outline or to generate some initial ideas that can then be worked up in further detail. Less experienced KM or legal practitioners may find this use case particularly helpful in getting them started with a thorny problem.

A further use case for AI in the "think" category is as a "thought partner". It can be particularly powerful to use an AI tool to stress-test your ideas and initial drafts, in a similar way that you might ask a colleague to try to pick holes in your drafting or legal arguments. It can also critique and improve a first draft and suggest additions and enhancements to material that you have generated. While it may not be an intuitive first choice for applying genAI, many legal practitioners have found applications of this type to be extremely helpful.

Write

The final component is "write". Here again, there may be some caution in applying genAI technology, especially to technical legal processes. However, genAI is specifically designed to generate output, so in principle it is ideally suited to this element of legal work and can add significant value. While some KM and legal professionals might doubt the ability of AI tools to produce accurate and reliable legal content, the legally-trained LLMs are already highly adept at this and are only going to improve further over time.

AI technology, therefore, can potentially support the generation of a wide range of material – from a non-technical summary of a legal document to thought leadership material, marketing collateral, or specific wording for an agreement or other document with legal effect.

The remainder of this chapter is devoted to exploring some practical examples of where genAI tools can support KM and legal professionals in their work. Of course, this is by no means an exhaustive list; rather, it is a series of examples to consider based on the framework outlined above.

Tasks focused on reviewing

Reviewing a new case, law or other document

GenAI could be used to review a new legal development, such as a new case, a piece of draft legislation, or a government discussion paper on a regulatory issue. The AI will be able to ingest the new information – largely irrespective of length and complexity – in a matter of seconds. In doing so, it can consider not only the sources on which it has been previously trained, but additional material from a range of different sources. Many tools can also ingest material in a wide variety of formats – not only documents, for example, but recordings of meetings, podcasts, and other media that would require a significant investment of time for human review. For example, a user could upload a consultation paper and a series of separate responses to the consultation from various industry bodies, or a new judgment alongside a podcast recorded by two leading experts discussing said judgment. Once ingested, the "think" and "write" capabilities can be used to query the material and/or to produce collateral based on the reviewed content. (See further below.)

Large-scale document reviews

This use case for machine learning, which involves training the tool on large sets of example documents so it can learn patterns and make predictions on others, has been well-established for a number of years. The business case strengthens significantly with a larger volume of documents: as the numbers go up, it quickly becomes too time-consuming and expensive to review an entire collection using human resources. Tasks such as identifying documents with particular characteristics (such as being privileged in the context of litigation, or containing a change of control clause in the context of a transaction) are, therefore, ideally suited to AI, with the added potential that a genAI tool can also create output based on an analysis of the content, such as a draft report highlighting the issues and risks found in the documents.

Extracting information

A related task is extracting information – either from a single document or from a collection of documents reviewed by the AI. As examples, the AI could extract all action items from a recording of a meeting; create a timeline from a series of witness statements and look for errors and inconsistencies; or pull out the conditions precedent from a loan agreement and format them in a table for easy reference.

Proofreading

Proofreading of various sorts is another good application for AI. For example, it can very quickly check that all cross-references and defined terms are correct, suggesting wording changes where necessary. It can also review a document for errors and inconsistencies or missing information. A good example of this is where multiple individuals have contributed to the drafting of a document, or where a number of source documents have been used to collate material for a single output document. In either situation, it is likely that the language used throughout the final document will have become inconsistent, and these points can quickly and easily be identified – and, if necessary, ironed out – by an AI tool.

Comparing two documents at a semantic level

Tools to compare two text-based documents have been existent for several decades, but these comparisons are based on a literal word-by-word and letter-by-letter comparison between one document and another. While many of today's tools will perform sophisticated comparisons and, for example, identify text that has been moved, rather than marking the change twice as both a deletion and an addition, they are still carrying out a direct textual comparison. GenAI tools, however, can compare the *effect* of each clause of the document at a conceptual level, flagging additions and deletions, and simultaneously note that some clauses may have an identical or similar legal effect, but are worded completely differently. To give a simple example, two clauses reading "This contract will terminate on 31 December 2026" and "This agreement shall end on December 31st, 2026" will be treated as different by a text-based comparison tool, but as the same by an AI tool performing a semantic comparison.

This capability is potentially even more valuable in the case of multiple document comparisons, which traditional text comparison tools tend not to do very well. An AI tool will be able to identify at a conceptual level which documents are similar and which are outliers, and to flag the substantive differences between them, irrespective of the drafting style or the precise wording used.

Classifying know-how

A task that has traditionally been the mainstay of many knowledge professionals is the classification of knowledge material, such as sample work product, training materials, and client briefings. It is a painstaking task that involves completing a series of metadata fields to describe each item of know-how. This additional metadata is invaluable for lawyers who are seeking to retrieve content by searching or browsing to find relevant material. Without detailed and accurate metadata, a know-how collection of even relatively modest size becomes impossible to navigate effectively.

This task has faced the traditional challenges: it is very labor-intensive and time-consuming, and even highly skilled individuals often struggle to achieve a high degree of consistency when adding metadata to content. All these problems can now be addressed using an AI, which can tag documents both quickly and consistently. It is worth mentioning that this ability does not obviate the need for a well-structured taxonomy. In fact, it makes it more important than ever, because AI needs a reliable framework to produce consistent metadata. The AI tool will only be able to tag content accurately if it is given a clear taxonomic structure to use for classification purposes.

Tasks involving analysis

User queries

Material that has been uploaded and analyzed – whether this be a new development, a draft agreement, or a piece of internal know-how – can then be queried by users through the AI's chat interface. In effect, users can question the AI about the underlying material. Depending on their level of expertise, this could range from simple explanations to much more in-depth analyses. For example, a user might ask the following:

- Explain the effect of Clause 8 of the agreement;

- Describe in bullet points how the government's position has changed since the last consultation on this topic;
- Summarize the financial implications of this new law for clients in the hospitality industry in 3–5 short bullet points as a briefing for the finance director of a national hotel chain; and
- Outline which other warranties would normally be included in an agreement of this type.

Some of these example prompts are better than others, but all will produce usable output. In most cases, users will want to review and verify the output from the AI. Many tools on the market today will not only provide an answer to any prompt, but will also offer citations to support their answer, as well as references to specific sections of the document. This will enable even relatively junior individuals to check the answer provided in most cases.

Informal training

By using the AI as described above to answer user questions, it can easily become an informal training tool, especially for junior professionals. One of the concerns or criticisms often cited regarding the use of AI in a legal context is that it will involve "de-skilling" lawyers. How will they learn their trade, the question goes, if the AI does much of the reading, analysis, and drafting for them?

In reality, this should not be a concern, because AI can itself become a training tool. Indeed, by providing a safe environment in which juniors can ask any question without fear of appearing foolish in front of their more experienced colleagues, there is a strong argument to suggest that, far from de-skilling them, AI will in fact support the *up*skilling of lawyers and KM professionals.

A "thought partner"

A particularly effective use of genAI can be in helping to refine thinking. By using the AI as a thought partner to help review, analyze, test, pick holes in, and augment legal analyses and arguments, users can often create much more sophisticated output than they would be able to do on their own. Interacting with an AI in this way can be thought of as consulting with a group of highly knowledgeable and experienced colleagues.

One example might be writing a piece of thought leadership, which analyzes the implications of a new legal development. Using an AI tool to think through the impact can be a very effective way of crafting an insightful analysis. Similarly, using the AI to critique your own first draft of a document and to suggest ways in which it could be improved will almost always yield useful insights.

Another example would be asking the AI to review an amended draft document to identify the changes, and comment on them, and suggest alternative wording. Equally, in the context of a transaction or of a dispute, it could put forward arguments to support your case or counterarguments in relation to the other side's points.

Analyzing usage statistics

Much KM work nowadays is systems-driven, so it is important to understand how users are interacting with relevant systems and to be able to draw conclusions from that understanding. This is another area in which AI can assist: by providing the tool with usage data, it will be able to analyze who is using the tool and how it is being used, and draw inferences from the data, such as content gaps; content that should be more heavily promoted; and content that needs to be reviewed for accuracy and relevance.

Identifying trends over time

One category of tasks that is extremely difficult for humans to perform is to identify trends – such as changes in market practice – that manifest themselves over an extended period of time. These insights are often extremely valuable as a source of market intelligence, but are difficult to identify using traditional means. In a transactional context, for example, there may be great value in being able to identify clauses that tend to be more heavily negotiated; warranties that tend to be rarely accepted; or new provisions that tend to be requested by counterparties. Insights of this nature, which a genAI tool can easily generate when provided with the right background materials and information, can be fed back into internal or client training programs, templates, and other internal knowledge products or thought leadership and other market-facing collateral.

Tasks focused on drafting

Drafting a summary targeted at a particular readership

Having ingested material uploaded by the user, one effective capability of genAI is to produce a succinct summary of that material. With thoughtful prompting, the output can be tailored to focus on particular areas of interest and targeted at a particular audience. For example, the AI could be prompted to produce a summary of a new legal development in the form of a client briefing of between 800–1,000 words in length, focusing on the implications of the new development for in-house lawyers in the pharmaceutical sector, with particular emphasis on the new product labelling requirements.

Alternatively, the AI could produce a series of topics, with talking points to be used by experts for a podcast, or a short blog entry highlighting one key development. Once again, a more structured prompt will almost always result in a higher quality, more tailored output.

Creating a draft template or standard form document

Having ingested a reasonable number of good examples of a particular type of document – a commercial lease, for example – the AI could then be prompted to create a standard form template based on those examples. With detailed prompting, the tool could include language that is common to all (or most) examples; it could add optional wording – such as a guarantee and the associated definitions – to cover the different scenarios represented by the varying examples provided, potentially with footnotes providing guidance on when the relevant wording should be used; and it could include links to relevant external materials.

If the genAI tool has access to relevant legal knowledge, it will be able to draw on these to produce a better output. The quality of the output will also depend on the number and quality of the samples provided, as well as the sophistication of the prompt. It is unlikely to produce a completely finished draft of a template that is immediately ready for lawyer consumption, except perhaps in the case of a very simple document, but it certainly has the potential to save KM professionals a huge amount of time in one of their core areas of work.

Creating a document based on another

A similar use case involves asking the AI to draft a document based on other inputs, such as a term sheet and a template. This task involves making appropriate changes to the template document based on the information contained in the term sheet. Another example might be asking the AI to draft a secondary transaction document from an agreement drafted previously, such as a security document in relation to a financing transaction, based on the loan agreement.

Preparing training materials

Another drafting-heavy task could be to create a set of training materials – perhaps in the form of a slide deck or a case study – from a series of notes, a recorded discussion, or some other content source. Uploading the background materials and then prompting the AI to generate output in the desired format may not produce a 100 percent finished product; however, with structured prompting, it will likely be a good starting point and almost certainly will save you time.

Translation from and into other languages

Although publicly available tools such as Google Translate have been in existence for nearly 20 years, the ability of genAI tools – especially those based on an LLM that has been trained on legal content – to read, ingest, and analyze legal information makes them ideally suited for translating material between languages. This application can be particularly useful for individuals who work in international firms or who deal with legal issues outside of the UK and/or in languages other than English. As noted above, a user can also use the AI to explain unfamiliar concepts or improve their understanding of the document by asking questions via the chat interface.

Drafting a communication

Less of a specialist legal application, but a significant potential timesaver nevertheless, AI can also be used to draft communications of various kinds. For example, given some rough notes and underlying materials, an AI could quickly draft an email that needs to be tactfully worded and explain some technical legal issues in layman's terms. Similarly, it could create a more formal letter for a client or create output in a particular style. Users can also interact with the AI to adjust the language accordingly – for example, by asking it to shorten certain sections; expand on a few specific points; or change the tone to fit the intended audience better. It is worth remembering that the first output does not need to be the final product, but can instead be refined by the AI – through multiple iterations, if necessary.

Amending existing drafting

Another potential use of a genAI tool is to amend existing drafting, such as the wording in a template document or an agreement drafted for an ongoing transaction. GenAI allows users to make wholesale conceptual changes via the chat interface without having to undertake the detailed drafting themselves. For example, the AI could be instructed to make the wording of a particular clause more balanced or more favorable to one of the parties. Alternatively, it could be asked to make more radical changes to a document by bringing in a new provision or set of provisions – such as adding a guarantee and the associated definitions – into a draft agreement.

Conclusions

The potential of genAI to transform the way in which KM and legal professionals work is hard to overstate. The examples provided above indicate the impressive capabilities that many of the tools available on the market already demonstrate, and sceptics should remember that this technology is still – relatively speaking – in its infancy, so it is only going to get better and more capable going forward. Hopefully, this chapter has provided some inspiration for the creative thinking that will be needed for the legal knowledge profession fully to harness the potential of this technology.

Chapter 3:

Building a strong foundation for AI application: ensuring data quality and integrity

By Grant Newton, lead consultant, Atlas by ClearPeople, and Sarah Pullin, global director of knowledge, Baker McKenzie

Artificial intelligence (AI) tools offer substantive transformative potential for legal knowledge management (KM), such as reducing research time, increasing overall discoverability of useful content, increasing understanding and tagging of content, and reducing time to complete document reviews. To achieve a successful transformation, AI is reliant on a culture that promotes a strategic and consistent approach to collective intelligence, rather than individual or inconsistent attitudes to developing, retaining, and sharing knowledge. If a firm does not embrace a top-down data-ready culture, the firm-wide quality and integrity of the data will therefore be questionable, and results from AI tools will be inconsistent and unreliable. The success of AI-based tools does depend on the quality and integrity of the data it uses. If the quality of data is suboptimal – whether that means the data are incomplete, inconsistent, outdated, or biased – it may likely lead to inaccurate outputs, ethical breaches, and reputational harm. This chapter explains why the quality and integrity of data is essential to AI adoption in law firms, how to achieve it, and the governance frameworks that are required.

Why data quality and integrity matters

The paradigm for successful searching and analysis is the same for AI: they are all reliant on the quality of the data available. To be "AI-ready" means an organization needs to be "data-ready for AI". Organizations are, therefore, beginning to redesign workflows, implementing governance and risk mitigation to generate value from AI investments.[1] The reason underlying this change is the acknowledgment that poor quality data will undermine AI accuracy, create compliance risks, and erode trust in the outcomes. To address data quality, it is important to understand what "quality and integrity" means, and how these qualities may vary based on the type of data.

Defining quality and integrity

Defining what is meant by quality and integrity will help people to understand how to use AI tools and their expectation of responses. An appreciation of the data available and their context and nature will drive behavior and will reduce the risk of inaccurate use. An understanding of what data the AI has used to produce an output helps to improve transparency and explainability, even if a person does not understand how the AI tool works. Transparency relates to how much information is shared about an AI tool and what it produces, whereas explainability and interpretability is about showing how an AI tool works behind the scenes and about making sense of the AI's results in terms of what the tool was designed to do.[2] This becomes particularly important when using a large language model (LLM) provided as a "black box" experience. Search engines suffer from the same trust issue in instances when it is not clear how the ranking algorithm determines what are the most relevant results to display first. Explainability is important when building trust in AI.[3]

Using targeted, clearly defined data collections based on specific AI use cases will improve transparency and explainability, even if the underlying mechanisms of how the AI tool works are not fully understood. When creating a dataset for an AI use case, consider the following dimensions:

Figure 1: Quality and integrity dimensions

Accuracy How auditable and accurate is the content that is included?	**Consistency** How consistent or diverse is the content in terms of its purpose?	**Completeness** How large is the source content that is in the scope of the AI tool?
Timeliness How current is the content and how often is it subject to change?	**Validity** How consistent are the data in terms of their structure and definition?	**Trustworthiness** How representative is the collection of the subject in question?

- **Accuracy:** Curated content that has been through rigorous review and refinement processes provides a trusted source of content that can be used verbatim. Citations are not useful if the source is not trusted, incorrect, irrelevant, or unknown.

- **Consistency:** A collection of content that has a specific purpose means that all content could potentially be relevant to the query unless specificity is addressed in the question asked, whereas diverse content could result in vague responses as irrelevant content gets inadvertently included.
- **Completeness:** If limited context is provided in the AI query, a large dataset means it then needs to assess and analyze more data prior to providing a response. Larger volume sets can also be subject to inconsistencies in the structure and are less likely to have consistent metadata across the collection, which will also directly impact relevancy of responses.
- **Timeliness:** Content that becomes obsolete or has timebound validity should be removed from the scope of the AI to reduce the risk of its inclusion. Content that is continually changing will affect the consistency of responses provided.
- **Validity:** It is important to understand the type of content that the AI is using to respond to the query provided. An appreciation of how it is defined and how consistent that structure and completeness of the metadata across the collection will inform both how the question may be asked and the responses provided.
- **Trustworthiness:** A collection that is missing differing viewpoints can result in biased output or incomplete responses that then proliferate the continued bias.

Types of legal data

The type of data and how they are structured forms part of the definition of data quality and how AI behaves when interrogating the content to respond to the question. Different types of data will inform the associated best practices in their curation and management.

Structured data

Structured data refers to organized information that is stored in well-defined formats, such as client details, matter information, and billing and time data. These data are, by their very nature, descriptive (ie, these are metadata) that, if correctly managed, can provide highly accurate responses. However, structured data are often siloed in systems inaccessible to AI tools, and decisions on how "openly" this content can be used must be addressed. Inconsistency in definitions, misaligned metadata, and duplications will impact AI outputs.

Best practices include:

- Implementing automated validation to detect and address anomalies;
- Applying de-duplication routines to maintain;
- Ensuring taxonomy consistency and alignment across systems;
- Aligning structured to unstructured data to provide greater context; and
- Using purpose-built AI tools to perform deep pattern and trend analysis, rather than general AI tools that are better suited to high-level sampling or comparative analysis.

Unstructured data

Unstructured data refers to information that has depth and breadth in context, but is difficult to standardize, such as contracts, pleadings, court transcripts, and precedents. These data can provide some of the most rewarding insights when using AI to gather, summarize, and semantically search across related content; however, AI is more prone to misinterpretation and elaboration beyond the original meaning towards hallucination when using these types of data.

Best practice includes:

- Using AI to propose metadata based on organizationally-defined taxonomy to improve and allow for "hashtag"-based retrieval, enabling AI query specificity based on a tag term;
- Defining rules for the AI to automatically apply metadata based on confidence levels set, deciding on a "level" of useful number of tags per term set, and continually reviewing to assess applicability;
- Applying multiple term sets, rather than having all terms as a single collection, so that the terms themselves can have relationships between term sets applied (for example, maintaining distinct Location and Department term sets);
- Ensuring that AI tools can query the content, assess content for keywords, and semantically match words to the organizational taxonomy, and review associated metadata to provide responses; and
- Standardizing common unstructured datasets into structured data, such as having common due diligence answers stored in a list/database to be used, instead of a document that is not clearly defined to respond to client questionnaires.

Tacit knowledge
Tacit knowledge is not strictly a type of datum, as it refers to the understanding that resides in experience and the practical application of the understood content, but it is important to consider how certain types of tacit knowledge can be translated into a useful dataset for AI. Examples may include transcripts from recordings, email threads, communities of practice conversations, and informal notes. These data, properly converted, can improve organizational effectiveness by making the knowledge accessible to a wider audience. Law firms risk losing institutional memory and limiting AI's ability to deliver nuanced outputs if this content is not captured and curated. This does have to be tempered with the risk that, without experience and appreciation, it could be incorrectly used.

Best practices include:

- Ensuring ownership is correctly attributed to the content – not necessarily to those who added or modified it, but to those who are the experts or the primary and contributing authors;
- Ensuring that, where it has not been through a curation process, it is clearly labelled using metadata of its "grading" (its level of peer review);
- Encouraging communities of practice to capture questions and best answers to common queries, so that this can be transformed into data that AI can better understand; and
- Providing mechanisms to easily capture this information and apply reasoning over the top of the content to provide context for the AI.

Data as a strategic asset

Treating data as a strategic asset shifts the perception of them as a historical record of evidence required for the completion of a matter and regulatory compliance to items that have value for future engagements. However, changing the purpose of use of this content with AI introduces the risks of potential inappropriate use of sensitive data and seemingly correct responses that are in fact inaccurate. To minimize these risks, AI accountability needs to be established across the firm. This can be done by enhancing existing organizational governance frameworks where they exist, or adopting and adapting an AI framework. Organizations have the chance to update outdated data and analytics governance practices to include AI as part of their improved governance program.[4]

To start, an AI, data, and information governance committee that is empowered to oversee AI governance is required. The responsibilities of an AI, data, and information governance committee will include:

- **Strategic alignment:** Ensure that AI initiatives aligned with business objectives.
- **Policy development:** Define standards for data quality, privacy, security, and ethical AI use.
- **Risk management:** Conduct bias audits, compliance checks, and scenario-planning.
- **Lifecycle governance:** Oversee model monitoring, retraining, and decommissioning. It should be noted that, where models are provided by third parties, the ability to influence retraining is unlikely and potentially not recommended, to avoid any risk of organizational data being used to train the model. Where external models are being used, knowing the model being used is important, alongside having an effective way to review and test changes in behaviors between models implemented.
- **Education and change management:** Continually improve AI literacy and accountability across the firm.
- **Ethical standards:** Embed fairness, privacy, and security into governance policies.
- **Security and regulatory oversight:** Ensure that the use of AI respects underlying system access permissions and is aligned with current jurisdictional AI regulations.

Once in place, the committee will be responsible for validating and approving an AI framework.

Principles for AI data governance

As part of the developing and delivering upon an AI framework, existing data governance principles will need to be updated to address the unique challenges that AI introduces.

Principles that should be considered include:

- **Accountability:** Assign clear decision rights for AI use cases, data stewardship, and compliance. Where data stewardship is responsible for the delivery of the policies set, consider the democratization of stewardship to the hands of the experts.
- **Transparency:** Ensure output from AI models and data collections is auditable and explainable. Where AI models are provided by third parties, the focus for a law firm becomes more on the data collection itself, while setting transparency requirements for the third party.

- **Lifecycle oversight:** Monitor AI models for drift, bias, and performance throughout their lifecycle. Again, the importance of data quality based on the above dimensions will help in instances where a law firm is using a third-party model. Keeping the data relevant to the purpose of the use case will minimize issues of model drift and bias.
- **Cross-functional collaboration:** Include legal, compliance, IT, data science/analysis, and KM stakeholders. Cross-functional teams should be empowered to implement standards, monitor compliance and manage the data lifecycle for use cases that they are responsible for.
- **Taxonomy alignment and metadata standards:** Align taxonomy terms, definitions, and relationships and define mandatory fields across systems where data may be used by AI to respond. Ensure that taxonomy and metadata are consistently applied.

Providing clear principles for AI data governance provides the "guardrails" people need for appropriate AI use. By adopting a set of data governance principles, an international law firm was able to achieve:

> *"A taxonomy overhaul across platforms and alignment with market-leading external taxonomies [which] resulted in the reclassification of 44,000 documents, enhancing discoverability, strategic alignment, and scalability. Governance was formalized through a dedicated committee, ensuring accountability and lifecycle oversight."*

Creating an AI-ready data strategy

Knowledge comprises both structured data and unstructured content. Separately or combined, the different types of information offer value, but simultaneously present distinct challenges for AI adoption. To build a strong foundation for AI tools, law firms need to integrate these data types into a logical architecture supported by governance, automation, and human oversight.

Potential challenges include:

- Structured data are easier to validate, but can be limited in context – for example, billable hours recorded will confirm time spent, but will explain little about the associated complexity of the matter; and
- Unstructured data can be rich in context and legal reasoning, but this makes it harder to process and verify and can overwhelm the AI to the extent that it is unable to provide complete responses.

Potential risks include:

- Data that may present as structured are treated as unstructured data by the AI when processing, such as spreadsheets with content without any definitions applied;
- AI only uses a sample of the available data when asked to provide a count or reviews "all" cases, resulting in an incorrect response;
- The effort to verify and validate the response provided by AI takes longer than completing the research using search functionality and discussion with the experts involved;
- AI cannot provide precise responses as the source documents lack context, such as headers and paragraph numbering; and
- The data have permissions applied in such a way that the AI returns different responses based on the privileges of the person asking the question.

To address these challenges and risks, an AI-ready data strategy requires:

- **Technical due diligence:** Define use cases, functional needs, and compliance obligations and validate AI tools using sample/controlled understood datasets to test for accuracy and bias and ensure that audit trails to track use are supported. Identify how the AI tools will interact with systems and data.
- **Continuous data improvement:** AI supports the concept of continuous improvement and feedback loops if properly managed. Have a repeatable test pattern that can be used to assess the continued relevancy of responses and updates to the model to further refine and improve. Regularly validate AI outputs against human-reviewed benchmarks.
- **Prioritized use cases:** Focus on high-value or -cost tasks where automation is not possible and where the content is clearly defined, combined with low difficulty to deliver, such as initial compliance response, contract review, and response to tenders.
- **Data stewardship and best practices:** Educate subject matter experts on how best to use AI, so that they become collection owners, and ensure that the owners of different collections can learn from each other's success and failures.
- **Standardized data creation and collection processes:** Develop authoritative templates, precedents, and structured repositories for specific knowledge collections to provide consistency in how AI responds.
- **Enhanced data curation and grading processes:** Organize and grade

content using consistent taxonomies, contextual tagging, and grading of the authoritative nature of content.

- **Ongoing data review and retirement processes:** Ensure that data remain "fresh" and "relevant" based on their purpose and life expectancy.
- **Consistent data collections for AI:** Organize knowledge collections around role and responsibility, so that they are aligned with the underlying data repositories.
- **Alignment of taxonomy across systems:** Ensure consistent understanding and use of taxonomy across systems and collections to improve AI responses.
- **Automated data improvement where sensible:** Use AI to automate low-risk, high-volume activities that can be done with minimal human verification or can improve the quality of the input to be used by AI to respond to human-led research.
- **Continued human involvement:** Where opinion and expert judgment is required, AI should be used to support – and not replace – humans.

Practical steps for data quality management

AI can only deliver accurate, reliable outputs when provided with quality data. Poor data quality, whether outdated, incomplete, or inconsistently tagged, undermines AI performance and exposes firms to compliance risks. Attorneys must understand the limitations of AI tools.[5] Reduction of the risks associated with AI use requires data to be maintained across their lifecycle. Below are some practical steps law firms should adopt to manage the data lifecycle:

Figure 2: Example knowledge data management lifecycle

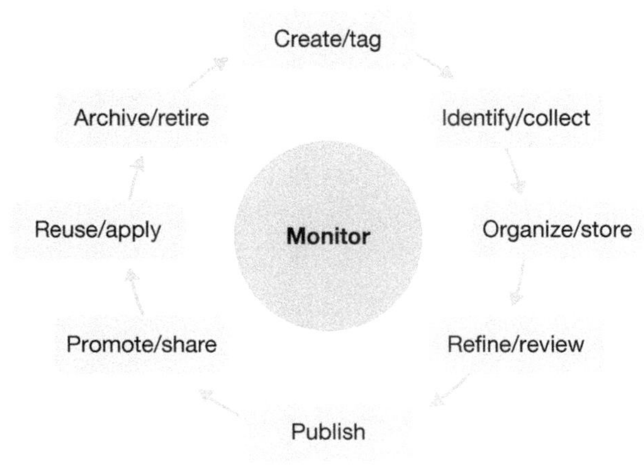

Quality standards and assurance

Quality standards define the principles for how best to define the quality and integrity of the data. Quality assurance is related to how the standards are monitored, maintained, and improved. Without clear standards and an approach to delivery, law firms cannot measure or enforce data quality.

Methods to establish robust quality standards include:

- Establishing data standards based on type and purpose of the data that take into consideration the quality and integrity dimensions applicable to AI use cases. Consider adopting an existing data management framework.[6]
- Defining a set of controls to address the delivery and management for data quality to:
  - Stop errors occurring at source;
  - Find and correct existing issues;
  - Prevent recurrence; and
  - Set metrics to monitor the success of activities.
- Setting measures to assess quality standards, such as:
  - An acceptable error rate to address accuracy;
  - A target for null values for completeness;
  - Acceptable data inactivity rates based on type of content, grading, and review cycles to manage timeliness; and
  - A target for duplication and conflicts across datasets for consistency.
- Agreeing what authoritative systems should be used as the "source of truth" and for which data.
- Agreeing taxonomy and metadata principles that can be applied across systems.
- Defining what metadata is required for which data and configuring KM systems to apply before content is saved.
- Applying reviews for high-value content and checking for completeness during these review cycles.
- Applying automation (where applicable) to:
  - Identify anomalies, incorrect formats, or outliers;
  - Correct errors and remove duplicates before including them in collections used by AI; and
  - Track and review missing fields, empty columns, and incomplete records.

Tagging and profiling

Tagging and profiling means applying metadata to content to improve contextual search and AI retrieval. Using taxonomies and metadata, an AI tool can be enabled to apply semantic and keyword understanding to the question asked and include associated synonyms to the terms in the query. Metadata management is a critical discipline that can help to unlock AI's potential.[7]

To achieve this:

- Define a controlled set of taxonomy and metadata columns, such as jurisdiction, matter type, sectors, subject and confidentiality levels;
- Automate tagging based on where content is saved and introduce AI assisted tagging based on the organization's taxonomy; and
- Validate profiling completeness of collections and address gaps.

Content review

Content review ensures that knowledge assets remain current, relevant, and aligned with the law firm's strategy. Outdated and legislatively incorrect knowledge can mislead AI models, resulting in inaccurate outputs and reputational harm. Steps to achieve an effective content review process includes:

- Introducing review cycles based on the nature of the content to check its relevance and currency;
- Providing definitions of what review dates mean and how they impact the relevance of the content;
- Reviewing and reassigning ownership of content when people join, leave, or retire;
- Scheduling periodic reviews with clear ownership and accountability;
- Ensuring that version control is used to manage and track previously correct data, but is not included in AI responses;
- Including cover sheets for highly curated content that explains the purpose, assessment, review cycle, and experts associated;
- Indicating clearly the review process for content, so that people and AI can understand its currency;
- Creating dashboards to track review cycles and flag content that is overdue for review; and
- Temporarily removing/hiding content that is overdue for review from search and AI until updated.

Content grading and levels

To ensure people can easily identify authoritative sources, law firms should implement a tiered grading system for curated knowledge assets. This approach categorizes content based on its level of validation and strategic importance. It also supports the different content review cycles, so that important "gold standard" content is subject to more thorough and regular reviews. Grading definition supports trust and transparency in AI outputs. When combined with metadata tagging, it enables dynamic filtering, so that people can choose whether to see only highly curated authoritative content or include broader context as well.

Steps to achieve this are as follows:

- Introduce clear grading standards with definitions that are applicable;
- Display grading indicators in KM platforms and AI tools;
- Limit who can set the highest standards;
- Ensure an approval process is in place to publish highly curated content; and
- Provide AI collections with the ability to prioritize highly curated content.

Examples of grading include:

- **Gold (Advice):** Curated, vetted, approved by subject matter experts, and aligned with firm-wide standards, such as official templates and precedents that may be used for drafting and advisory outputs.
- **Silver (Guidance):** Reviewed for accuracy and relevance but may not be globally standardized or have been assessed for specific legal advice, such as practice guidance notes, awareness of regulatory changes, expert opinion, or simply factual content that may be used for contextual insights and secondary references.
- **Bronze (Information):** Informal or unverified content, such as discussion notes or exploratory drafts that may be useful as conjecture or assisting in understanding but should not be used as authoritative legal opinion of the firm.

Content archiving and retention

Archiving and retention involves removing outdated or irrelative content and applying retention schedules aligned with regulatory requirements. People naturally gravitate to a "keep everything" mentality as data became easier to keep for relatively low costs, leading to large inconsistent datasets and compliance risks. Data governance requires sensible retention strategies that balance accessibility with risk mitigation. These strategies include:

- Implementing automated archiving cycles to identify and remove obsolete content;
- Allowing for manual archiving so that data stewards can easily assess and remove "noise" content as and when needed;
- Aligning retention policies with jurisdictional requirements, such as GDPR and HIPAA;
- Clearly explaining and setting retention policies against all content;
- Managing retention as part of data, security, and risk management policies; and
- Monitoring for content that is copied/duplicated from the original copy to ensure that it retains the original retention label, unless authorization is provided to change.

An international law firm introduced a fundamental change in the approach to content and data management to address this issue by reviewing internal knowledge, which led to an "archiving of 59 percent of content and the launch of an automated bi-annual archiving process. This dramatically reduced outdated, low-value, and duplicative content, improving relevance and operational efficiency."

Content use tracking

Tracking how knowledge assets are accessed via AI tools, search, or browsing will provide insights into relevance, adoption, and gaps in the knowledge available. Without usage analytics, firms cannot measure success of KM initiatives, evaluate AI use, or identify underutilized content that may need review or promotion. Tracking strategies include:

- Monitoring content the AI tools reference and surface for the response;
- Reviewing what content the AI tools use and do not use to respond and reference;
- Capturing views to source materials cited in AI tool responses;
- Reviewing the queries being asked of the AI tools to understand what content is likely to be relevant; and
- Implementing feedback loops for people to highlight missing or incorrect data and responses.

Risk management and compliance

With the use of AI for KM and assessments of content, law firms must embed risk management and compliance into the data strategy to protect client confidentiality, uphold ethical standards, and maintain trust. AI tools can amplify the risks associated with poor data governance, as inaccurate and incorrectly classified content will result in inadequate responses or cross-pollination of data. If access control policies and sensitivity labels are not consistently applied across the data, they then risk exposing secure data breaching professional obligations. Failure to verify AI outputs or secure client data can represent a breach of professional duties, and courts have sanctioned attorneys for submitting hallucinated AI-generated content, as seen in *Mata v. Avianca*, reinforcing the need for rigorous oversight.[8] To address this risk, law firms should assess the following aspects and mitigate accordingly.

Legal and regulatory

Legal professionals need to ensure they understand the potential impact on data privacy laws, client confidentiality, and cross-border data-sharing when using AI tools. Vital components of a good legal and regulatory assessment include:

- Maintaining a compliance register mapping applicable regulations to internal policies;
- Making the register available in a format that enables search and AI to easily access the rules in place;
- Conducting periodic audits to verify adherence to retention schedules and privacy requirements; and
- Implementing legal holds for eDiscovery to preserve relevant content.

Security challenges

Ensuring content is consistently secured across multiple repositories and platforms is an existing security risk. Understanding how content moves between systems and what content the AI tools are using to respond is now also critical to managing a global access control model. This challenge is very similar to that of enterprise search tools. To address these challenges, you must:

- Validate what sources are being used by the AI tools and ensure that the same security model is applied;
- Manage access to AI collections through a central identity management system; and

- Maintain audit trails for all data interactions for AI-generated responses.

Version control

AI tools should only access the most recent approved version of a document. Redundant, outdated, and incorrect content should also be excluded. To achieve this, you should:

- Maintain authoritative versioning protocols in applicable systems;
- Ensure that AI collections only use authoritative sources rather than "everything";
- Apply lifecycles to archive obsolete documents while preserving auditability; and
- Monitor for copies and duplication of older versions to ensure retention and use guidelines are still applied.

Auditability and transparency

Transparent data handling processes and AI inference and outputs are essential for trust and defensibility in legal contexts. To ensure transparency, you should:

- Ensure data lineage and traceability is implemented to track data source, any transformations applied and its usage;
- Document AI model testing datasets and validation procedures; and
- Periodically assess AI collections to understand source content being used and its associated permissions, retention policies, and sensitivity levels.

Sensitivity labels

Sensitivity labels define how and when content can be used, especially when AI tools collate or process sensitive information. These labels help people to understand the sensitivity of the content that they have permissions to access. Providing users with guidance on where the content can be safely used can be achieved by:

- Creating a sensitivity classification framework with labelled tiers such as Public, Internal, Confidential, Client-Privileged, and Regulatory-Sensitive;
- Ensuring that AI tools include these labels in the output and clearly highlight what elements of the response have used differently labelled content;

- Reducing risk by creating AI collections that only contain one tier of sensitivity, rather than a mix;
- Including instructions in the AI collections that highlight potential risks associated with using and sharing responses, based on any highly sensitive content included;
- Ensuring sensitivity labels are enforced on content creation and are automatically reviewed based on metadata and content scanning to address incorrect labelling; and
- Tracking label application and usage patterns to ensure compliance with firm policies and client agreements.

Permission and access control

Permissions and access control manage what an individual can access using search and AI. AI should respect permissions and ethical walls (information barriers) that are in place. Permission management reduces the risk of unauthorized sharing of data and supports adherence to compliance obligations. To implement an effective permission management strategy, you should:

- Create AI collections that align with groups that have similar access to the underlying dataset;
- Ensure that autonomous agents are not provided with incorrectly elevated permissions;
- Assign permissions based on roles and functions;
- Provide appropriate guidance when using an AI tool with permissioned content;
- Educate people on governance policies and ethical use of AI;
- Maintain audit logs of who accessed what, when, and why; and
- Use compliance dashboards to monitor access patterns and detect anomalies.

Ethical and regulatory considerations

The use of AI has not changed the ethical and regulatory obligations for law firms. Attorneys remain responsible for the accuracy, competence, and integrity of all work, regardless of the tools employed. AI tools can be used to assist with research, drafting, and analysis, but attorneys cannot abdicate responsibility for verifying outputs.

Verification of responses

All AI responses must be verified and checked to ensure that they comprise a correct interpretation and representation of the underlying content. It is important not to underestimate the potential effort involved in verifying AI responses, as the potential effort may start to outweigh the value unless properly managed through data quality initiatives that affect how the AI tool validates its sources.[9] A good data quality initiative includes:

- Using AI tools that provide links to the source content and the exact extracts used to respond;
- Using specialized curated data collections where specificity is required for legal research;
- Ensuring that all AI responses are verified by a person and approved by an expert;
- Implementing validation protocols that are appropriate to the risk of the process; and
- Checking all citations to ensure they are accurate.

Confidentiality and informed consent

The use of AI to create responses and the potential for data to be used to train models has meant that clients are placing controls on its use when it comes to using their data and delivering work. Understanding what controls are in place and how best to comply is essential. To achieve this, you should:

- Review and maintain details of AI obligations stated in clients outside counsel guidance agreements;
- Disclose to clients where AI is used;
- Ensure that privileged content is flagged using sensitivity labels, and that collections used by AI are clearly flagged based on data classifications;
- Verify and assess if the AI tool used has access to train its model based on the firm's dataset and manage accordingly;
- Restrict AI training datasets to anonymized or non-confidential material where applicable; and
- Consider using redaction techniques to remove personally identifiable information and protected information from the data.

Bias and fairness

AI tools can extend or amplify bias present in data, posing ethical and reputational risks. If data used to either train or respond to queries are not representative, AI will tend to use this content exclusively. To address this, you should:

- Conduct bias audits during AI knowledge collection and model validation;
- Use diverse and representative datasets if training AI models; and
- Implement governance policies that ensure fairness and non-discrimination in AI-assisted processes.

Building a data-ready culture

Creating a strong foundation for AI in legal KM involves people, processes, and culture. Data quality and integrity cannot be delivered without organizational commitment to continuous improvement, ethical and collective responsibility, and adaptability. Sarah Pullin of Baker McKenzie notes that firms must ask:

> *"... how will this drive measurable value? That lens informs our approach to content and data quality, governance, and risk transparency, ensuring that our data and business systems are optimized for compliance and efficiency and primed for AI enablement."*[10]

Organizational change

Data governance must go beyond technical compliance and become a cultural norm. Accuracy, verification, and ethical responsibility into daily thinking. Organizations must balance robust governance with broad democratization – all managed through a product mindset.[11] Key actions include:

- Making data quality a shared responsibility across KM, IT, and legal teams;
- Establishing governance committees with clear accountability; and
- Communicating the strategic importance of data integrity through leadership messaging.

Training and leadership

Attorneys and KM professionals need to be upskilled in the use of AI tools. Training should include critical thinking, verification skills, and ethical reasoning. Leadership must champion these initiatives, allocate resources, and reinforce the message that human oversight remains indispensable. Key actions include:

- Developing AI literacy programs on risks, limitations, and governance;
- Providing workshops showing how to use AI tools; and
- Leading by example and prioritizing governance in strategic planning.

Collaboration and human oversight

Maintaining data quality requires collaboration between KM, IT, compliance, and legal teams. AI does not remove responsibility; human oversight is essential to deliver trusted outcomes. Key actions include:

- Forming cross-functional teams to work on specific use cases;
- Sharing insights to improve future use cases;
- Ensuring data quality and integrity is maintained throughout; and
- Increasing adoption through regular targeted communication.

Future-proofing and continuous improvement

AI is evolving rapidly; firms need adaptable strategies without compromising governance. Continuous feedback loops, audits, and scorecards help maintain accuracy and compliance. Key actions include:

- Creating a flexible data architecture for AI integration without compromising data sovereignty;
- Monitoring AI regulatory changes and adjusting governance accordingly;
- Establishing feedback loops to capture user insights and refine AI configurations;
- Conducting periodic audits to validate governance compliance; and
- Assessing usage to identify high-demand collections and retire obsolete data assets.

Conclusions

Providing a well-defined and clearly understood data foundation for the use of AI in legal KM is required for effective outcomes. To provide this stable data foundation, law firms will need to adopt a governance framework and implement standards for data creation, curation, and retention. Continuous improvement, collaboration across teams, and a culture of accountability are essential for sustaining trust and adaptability as AI technologies evolve. The success of AI relies on data quality available, and the associated integrity gained through consistently accurate responses.

References

1 Singla A, Sukharevsky A, Yee L et al, *The state of AI: How organizations are rewiring to capture value*, McKinsey & Company, March 2025. See: https://www.mckinsey.com/~/media/mckinsey/business%20functions/quantumblack/our%20insights/the%20state%20of%20ai/2025/the-state-of-ai-how-organizations-are-rewiring-to-capture-value_final.pdf.

2 Tabassi E, "Artificial Intelligence Risk Management Framework (AI RMF 1.0)", National Institute of Standards and Technology, 26 January 2023. See: https://www.nist.gov/publications/artificial-intelligence-risk-management-framework-ai-rmf-10.

3 Giovine C and Roberts R, "Building AI trust: The key role of explainability", McKinsey & Company, 26 November 2024. See: https://www.mckinsey.com/capabilities/quantumblack/our-insights/building-ai-trust-the-key-role-of-explainability.

4 Goasduff L, "Gartner Predicts 80% of D&A Governance Initiatives Will Fail by 2027, Due to a Lack of a Real or Manufactured Crisis", Gartner, 28 February 2024. See: https://www.gartner.com/en/newsroom/press-releases/2024-02-28-gartner-predicts-80-percent-of-data-and-analytics-governance-initiatives-will-fail-by-2027-due-to-a-lack-of-a-real-or-manufactured-crisis-.

5 American Bar Association, "ABA issues first ethics guidance on a lawyer's use of AI tools", 26 July 2024. See: https://www.americanbar.org/news/abanews/aba-news-archives/2024/07/aba-issues-first-ethics-guidance-ai-tools/.

6 Data management frameworks include the Data Administration Management Association's (DAMA) Data Management Body of Knowledge (https://dama.org/learning-resources/dama-data-management-body-of-knowledge-dmbok/) and the International Organization for Standardization's (ISO) ISO 8000-1:2022 – Data Quality (https://www.iso.org/standard/81745.html).

7 Gotts F, "Metadata Management: A Critical Discipline That Can Help Unlock AI", *Forbes*, 12 July 2024. See: https://www.forbes.com/councils/forbestechcouncil/2024/07/12/metadata-management-a-critical-discipline-that-can-help-unlock-ai/.

8 *Mata v. Avianca*, USDC SDNY, 22-cv-1461 (2023).

9 Yuvaraj J, "The Verification-Value Paradox: A Normative Critique of Gen AI in Legal Practice", *arXiv*, 23 October 2025. https://doi.org/10.48550/arXiv.2510.20109.

10 Austin C, Hirebet S, Karawani G and Pullin S, "Modern legal workflows: how human are they?", *Peer to Peer*, 2025, issue 2, volume 41. https://epubs.iltanet.org/i/1538025-summer25/21?.

11 Chaurasia J, Suiter A et al, *The Forrester Data And AI Governance Model*, Forrester, 17 July 2025. See: https://www.forrester.com/report/the-forrester-data-and-ai-governance-model/RES184942.

Chapter 4:
Making AI work for you (from the inside out)

By Mark Gediman, senior research analyst, Alston & Bird LLP, and Kevin Miles, library manager, Norton Rose Fulbright US LLP

As I investigate a particularly thorny subject, an email with the dreaded red exclamation point (!) hits my inbox. I save my online auction search (vintage pointed ears from my favorite science fiction television series!) and, with a sigh, open the email. A partner wants any information I can find for a pitch for a new litigation matter for an existing client. In addition to the usual research resources on Lexis, Westlaw, or Bloomberg Law, this will require checking internal resources as well. In particular, it is important to know if the firm has:

- Litigated cases against the plaintiff's law firm and/or their attorney;
- Had contact with the plaintiff's law firm and/or their attorney;
- Had cases before this judge; and
- Litigated similar cases generally and for this client.

For budgeting purposes, it would also be beneficial to know the cost of litigating similar cases in the past.

Internal databases can be a reliable source for these kinds of information. The document management system (DMS) contains the firm's work product for litigation and transactional matters, as well as correspondence. The contact relationship management system (CRM) is a good source for tracking contacts and interactions (no pun intended). Financial information can be found in finance or billing systems, using such tools as Foundation or Microsoft's Power BI.

Some firms have addressed the problem of searching multiple files with an enterprise search solution. Most of these products operate by linking a keyword search engine to various internal datasets. The typical result of searches on these enterprise searches is overwhelming. Hundreds or thousands of documents are retrieved from various sources. It is difficult to apply context to most of these search engines, resulting in large amounts of extraneous materials. Artificial intelligence (AI) promises to simplify searching through this mountain of information.

There are concerns with making these systems accessible to AI. AI access to proprietary and confidential business information creates a risk that these types of data will appear in search results outside the organization. AI systems also have a propensity to create false results in an effort to answer questions put to them. These issues can be addressed when implementing an AI system. A copy of the AI can be installed within a firm's network environment, preventing the information from leaking outside the firm. Making sure the AI product isn't linked or synchronized with external versions of the system is important to maintaining the confidentiality of your data. Emphasizing to the end users – both attorneys and staff – that AI should be a starting point to your research, not an end point, is important. Training in these systems should include a clear-eyed discussion of their drawbacks and is key to successful implementation.[1]

The search tools that are native to internal DMSs and financial databases are clunky at best and incomplete at worst. The search is word-based, and the results are inconsistent. The use of Boolean search connectors such as "and" "or" "w/N" and "/p" are typically not available in these search engines. The user is also limited to keyword or phrase searching, with a space interpreted as an "or", resulting in very large result sets that make it difficult to find relevant documents that meet the contextual needs of the research.

Some examples of use cases on the Copilot platform are included below. There are many varieties of AI platforms available for internal use. For the purposes of this chapter, these examples have been run using Copilot, as a tool most are familiar with. As you know, Microsoft includes Copilot in Outlook, Edge, Word, and Excel. We will start broadly and then narrow down to more focused reports.

Killing the "Does anyone know...?" email

These emails are a source of frustration for many attorneys. These are normally sent out when they are putting together a pitch for a new litigation matter and want to showcase the firm's prior experience with either a) the opposing counsel, b) the judge assigned to this case, c) similar cases, d) the general counsel or other executive on the interview panel, or e) a combination of all of these. These are all important data points for attorneys to be armed with when pitching new business. Unfortunately, these emails seldom elicit a response. This results in the attorney turning to the business development or research professionals in the firm for this information. This information is hiding in both external and internal systems. A search system that combines the two without receiving an overwhelming amount of data is the dream of every analyst. Even better would be the ability to run a single enterprise search of the internal databases without receiving thousands of results (not an exaggeration – I can't begin to count the number of times this has happened). The internal databases with relevant information would be the DMS (iManage, NetDocs, etc), the financial databases, and the CRM database (Salesforce, Interaction, etc).

Below are some examples of Copilot prompts and answers. Readers should note that some of these responses, replicated here for illustrative purposes, contained internal data that we are unable to display due to security and confidentiality considerations. Subjective internal data that could be useful for these kinds of reports and responses are **formatted in bold** in Boxes 1–10. Output from Copilot that originally contained the names of real persons, organizations, locations, and firms has been anonymized, as it is the principle – rather than the facts – of these examples that should be noted by the reader. Please feel free to try these sample prompts out on your own Copilot, keeping in mind that no prompt is valid for all use cases. The particular circumstances of your firm are unique and may require different approaches. Bearing this in mind, how would you craft these prompts?

Box 1. Judicial profile/firm experience

Task: Investigating prior telecom litigation before a particular judge

Since we do not have a specific firm to use to search for this information, a more generic prompt is used.

Generic prompt: Which firms have been successful in litigating telecom-related cases before Judge X in the Central District of California?

Prompt modified with internal information: **Which attorneys have experience litigating telecom-related cases before Judge X?**

Useful internal data sources: **DMS, financial database**

Generic results

Quick answer: Attorneys from firms such as AB&C, XY&Z, D&E,

and F&G have litigated major telecom-related cases before Judge X in the Central District of California. These include high-profile disputes over FRAND licensing of standard-essential patents and consumer class actions involving telecom companies.

Attorneys with telecom litigation experience before Judge X

Here are some of the key lawyers who have appeared in telecom-related cases in Judge X's courtroom:

- J Doe (AB&C)
  - Represented defendant in a landmark case on FRAND licensing.
  - Known for expertise in intellectual property and telecom standards litigation.
- J Roe (XY&Z)
  - Lead counsel for plaintiff in the same FRAND dispute.
  - Experienced in defending Asian handset manufacturers in US patent and licensing cases.
- JQ Public (D&E)
  - Litigated telecom patent disputes involving wireless standards before Judge X.
  - Frequently represents major technology and telecom companies in federal courts.
- Attorneys from F&G
  - Given Judge X's own past partnership at F&G, the firm has a long history of appearing before him.
  - Their telecom practice includes representing carriers and equipment makers in California litigation.

Why these attorneys matter

- Specialization in telecom standards: They handle disputes involving 4G/5G patents and licensing.
- Experience with Judge X's courtroom style: He is known for efficiency, tentative rulings, and narrowing issues early.
- Global litigation footprint: These attorneys represent multinational telecom corporations, aligning with the international scope of Judge X's docket.

Sources: Wikipedia/PlainSite/RPX Insight/docs.justia.com

Imagine a version of this report that's focused on the experience of your firm using actual internal data. That will give you an idea of the power of including internal databases with context in your research.

Box 2. Plaintiff's counsel/firm experience

Task: Investigating experience with plaintiff's counsel

Generic prompt: What law firms have experience with litigating product liability cases against MNO?

Prompt using internal information: What experience does Firm XY&Z have litigating product liability cases against MNO?

Direct answer: Several prominent defense firms have experience litigating against MNO in product liability cases. Because MNO is one of the largest plaintiff firms in the US (specializing in defective products, mass torts, and consumer injury claims), corporate defendants and manufacturers often retain national defense firms and other mass tort defense specialists to oppose them.

Firms experienced in product liability defense against MNO

- PQ&R LLP. Ranked highly in product liability, mass tort, and class action defense. Frequently defends pharmaceutical, medical device, and consumer product companies in cases where MNO represents plaintiffs.
- UA The Law Firm. National defense firm specializing in complex product liability litigation. Known for defending manufacturers of automobiles, medical devices, pharmaceuticals, and consumer goods against plaintiff firms like MNO.
- ST&U (not in the search results but widely recognized). A leading defense firm in product liability and mass torts, often opposing plaintiff firms in cases involving defective drugs, chemicals, and consumer products.
- J&K Strong. A product liability defense practice, particularly in pharmaceutical and medical device litigation. Frequently faces plaintiff firms like MNO in multidistrict litigation (MDL).

Context

- MNO's role: They represent injured consumers in defective product cases (eg, defective vehicles, exploding e-cigarettes, workplace machines, medical devices).
- Defense firms' role: Corporations and manufacturers accused in these suits retain large national defense firms to counter MNO's aggressive plaintiff strategies.
- Litigation setting: Many of these disputes occur in federal MDL or state mass tort proceedings, where MNO is often a lead plaintiff firm.

Why these firms matter

- Scale: MNO files thousands of product liability claims annually, requiring equally large defense firms.
- Expertise: Defense firms specialize in minimizing liability for manufacturers, often through scientific evidence and regulatory defenses.
- Track record: Firms like L&M and UA have established reputations for successfully defending against plaintiff firms in high-stakes product liability cases.

Copilot prompt

Would you like me to build a timeline of major product liability MDLs where MNO was a lead plaintiff firm and these defense firms opposed them, or a profile of defense strategies commonly used against MNO?

Sources: MNO/Martindale.com/The Legal 500/UA

AI in action: business development (BD) and competitive intelligence (CI)

A question we hear often is: should AI be used in competitive intelligence? Absolutely! As shown by the previous examples, AI can be helpful when sifting through large amounts of internal information. AI should be used in CI as a starting point. As you gain confidence over time, AI can help beyond a starting point. Copilot is great for creating checklists, charting laws, identifying trends, and summarizing long internal and external documents for CI reports. It is a utility that is improving all the time. Perhaps the most important element in AI is to make sure what was reported is actual, not a hallucination. Additionally, you should also consider the wording and sequencing of your prompts. Is the first prompt the best? Sometimes it is. It is also often the case that the answer to the first prompt may inspire additional questions or give you reasons to narrow or expand your next prompt.

The advantages of AI for business development and CI are numerous and include:

1. **Automated data collection and monitoring:** AI tools continuously scan competitor websites, social media, news, and market reports, consolidating data in real time.
   Example: AI agents monitor competitor product launches and pricing changes, alerting teams instantly to market shifts.
2. **Pattern recognition and trend analysis:** machine learning algorithms detect patterns and anomalies across massive datasets, revealing market trends and competitor strategies that manual analysis would miss
   Example: AI identifies emerging consumer preferences from social media sentiment.
3. **Predictive analytics for strategic foresight:** AI forecasts future market movements, competitor actions, and regulatory changes using historical and current data.
   Example: Tesla uses AI-powered predictive analytics to anticipate industry trends in electric vehicles, staying ahead in battery technology and autonomous driving.
4. **Enhanced decision-making:** AI synthesizes vast information streams into actionable insights, supporting faster, more informed strategic decisions.
   Example: Capital IQ Pro's AI-powered tools help analysts quickly interpret market data and competitor filings for investment decisions.
5. **Real-time competitive alerts:** AI platforms provide automated alerts when competitors introduce new products, change prices, or run promotions, enabling rapid response.
   Example: Amazon's AI-driven pricing engine dynamically adjusts prices based on competitor activity and demand, maintaining market leadership.
6. **Sentiment analysis:** Natural language processing (NLP) extracts meaning from unstructured text, such as customer reviews and social media, to gauge public perception of competitors.
   Example: Companies can leverage AI to analyze customer feedback and social trends, informing product development and marketing strategies.
7. **Automated reporting and visualization:** AI generates CI reports, visualizations, and dashboards, saving analysts time and improving clarity for stakeholders.
   Example: Microsoft Copilot in Word and Excel creates CI report templates, summarizes laws, and charts trends for research teams.

8. **Competitor profiling and benchmarking:** AI aggregates and analyzes competitor data, enabling detailed profiling and benchmarking against industry leaders.
   Example: Manifold Group's AI solution scans millions of websites to uncover insights about HR trends and cyber risks among competitors.
9. **Risk assessment and early warning:** AI identifies operational, regulatory, and reputational risks by analyzing diverse data sources, providing early warnings.
   Example: AI tools flag regulatory changes or negative sentiment that could impact a company's competitive position.
10. **Strategic collaboration and scenario planning:** AI agents act as virtual collaborators, helping teams brainstorm, simulate scenarios, and refine strategies with data-backed suggestions.
   Example: AI-powered platforms facilitate strategy development by connecting data points and offering actionable recommendations for leadership teams.

Boxes 3–10 contain some examples of the output from Copilot for typical CI queries. Creating a template from scratch is an underutilized capability of AI that can be useful for tasks related to CI. When looking at the examples below, consider: what would you suggest for additional prompts?

Box 3. Creating a template

Task: Creating a CI report format

Copilot: Creating from within Word and formatting for Word

Rationale: To create a general template

Prompt: Create a CI report template

CI report template

1. Executive summary
   - Brief overview of key findings
   - Strategic implications
   - Recommended actions

2. Objectives
    - Purpose of the report
    - Specific questions to be answered

3. Methodology
    - Sources of information (public, proprietary, interviews, etc.)
    - Data collection methods
    - Analysis techniques

4. Market overview
    - Industry trends
    - Market size and growth
    - Key drivers and challenges

5. Competitor profiles
    - Company overview
    - Financial performance
    - Product/service offerings
    - Market positioning
    - Recent developments (M&A, partnerships, launches)
    - SWOT analysis (Strengths, Weaknesses, Opportunities, Threats)

6. Comparative analysis
    - Product/service comparison table
    - Pricing strategies
    - Marketing and sales tactics
    - Customer base and target segments

7. Strategic insights
    - Opportunities for your organization
    - Threats from competitors
    - Gaps in the market
    - Potential responses

8. Recommendations
    - Actionable steps based on findings
    - Prioritization of initiatives

9. Appendices
    - Detailed data tables
    - Source list
    - Glossary of terms

Creating a state law survey for a specific practice area and limited by the firm's geographic coverage can be valuable in identifying possible areas for growth.

Box 4. Survey of state laws

Task: Summarizing data breach notification laws for the states of Texas, California, Illinois, and New York

Copilot: Creating from within Word and formatting for Word

Rationale: Your supervisor wants to know more about four states so she can adequately advise her client

Prompt: What are the state data breach notification laws for Texas, California, Illinois, and New York displayed in a tabular format?

Possible follow-up prompts: **Do we represent clients involved in data breach litigation in these states? Who are the partners involved?**

Data breach notification laws summary

State	Statute	Deadline for consumer notice	Government notice	Threshold for gov notice	Definition of personal info	Encryption safe harbor
Texas	Tex. Bus. & Com. Code §§ 521.002, 521.053	Without unreasonable delay, no later than 60 days after discovery	Notify attorney general	If 250+ residents affected	Name + SSN, DL#, financial info, health info	Yes, if encryption key not accessed

continued on next page

State	Statute	Deadline for consumer notice	Government notice	Threshold for gov notice	Definition of personal info	Encryption safe harbor
California	Cal. Civ. Code §§ 1798.29, 1798.82	30 days after discovery (effective 1 Jan 2026)	Notify attorney general	If 500+ residents affected	Name + SSN, DL#, financial info, medical info, biometric, genetic data, login credentials	Yes, if encryption key not accessed
Illinois	815 ILCS §§ 530/1–530/50	Most expedient time possible, without unreasonable delay	Notify attorney general	If 500+ residents affected	Name + SSN, DL#, financial info, medical info, health insurance info, biometric, login credentials	Yes, if encryption key not accessed
New York	N.Y. Gen. Bus. Law § 899-AA (SHIELD Act)	30 days after discovery	Notify attorney general, dept. of state, state police, DFS	All breaches (plus consumer reporting agencies if >5,000 residents)	Name + SSN, DL#, financial info, biometric, medical info, health insurance info, login credentials	Yes, if encryption key not accessed

Encryption exceptions

All four states (Texas, California, Illinois, and New York) provide an encryption safe harbor. This means that if the breached data was encrypted and the encryption key was not compromised, notification requirements do not apply. The intent is to reduce risk when strong encryption protects personal information.

Additionally, using AI to quickly find industry trends can be a tremendous time-saver.

Box 5. State-level business trends

Task: Identifying top business trends in Texas in 2025 and beyond

Copilot: Creating from within Word and formatting for Word

Rationale: Your supervisor wants to know how the trends are doing. Which trends provide more business for the firm?

Prompt: Identify the top business trends in Texas for 2025

Top business trends in Texas (2025)

#	Trend	Key data/insights
1	Corporate relocations and HQ growth	Texas won the Governor's Cup for the 13th year in a row, with 1,368 capital investment projects in 2024, more than double Illinois. Over 180 companies announced relocations or expansions in 2024–2025, with DFW topping the US list.
2	Energy sector resilience	Oil and gas remain strong drivers. Elevated oil prices from geopolitical tensions support high-wage employment. Texas continues to lead in fossil fuels while also expanding renewables.
3	Tech and start-up ecosystem	Texas startups raised $2.9B in Q1 2025, with mega-rounds in defense tech, robotics, and cybersecurity.
4	Construction and real estate boom	Texas leads the nation in construction spending, projected at $50.3B in 2025, driven by housing demand and commercial development. Rapid suburban growth is reshaping formerly rural areas.

continued on next page

#	Trend	Key data/insights
5	Healthcare and finance transformation	Hospitals saw profitability gains despite Medicaid cuts, while healthcare finance is investing in automation and digital tools. Legislative reforms continue to strengthen Texas's financial sector.
6	Population and labor force shifts	Slower in-migration is moderating job growth, but Texas still outpaces the national average with 1.5 percent employment growth forecast for 2025. Major metros remain magnets for talent.

Key takeaways

- Texas remains the #1 state for corporate relocations, with companies fleeing high-cost states like California and New York.
- The energy industry is still the backbone, but diversification into renewables and tech is accelerating.
- Tech start-ups are booming, with record venture capital inflows and AI, cloud, and data analytics leading growth.
- Construction spending is the highest in the nation, reflecting Texas's population boom and housing demand.
- Healthcare and finance sectors are adapting with digital transformation, while policy reforms keep Texas competitive.

Copilot prompt

Would you like me to map these trends city by city (Dallas, Houston, Austin, San Antonio) so you can see how each metro contributes to Texas's overall business outlook?

Sources: businessintexas.com/Federal Reserve Bank of Dallas/Comerica/CandysDirt.com/JD Supra/Crunchbase News/kaviglobal.com/PlaceMKR Local Profile

Creating contact lists for target companies that meet specific criteria is a good use of AI. Those contacts can then be run against the internal databases for internal connections to these contacts.

Box 6. Top client analysis

Identifying top Dallas client companies by revenue and listing key executives

Copilot: Creating from within Word and formatting for Word

Rationale: Your supervisor wants to approach the top officers to cross-sell additional business

Possible prompt: Identify the top-grossing companies in Dallas, Texas, as well as the chairman, president, and general counsel of each company

Follow-up prompt: **Identify any attorneys within the firm that may have a relationship with these individuals**

Here's a snapshot of the top Dallas-based companies ranked by revenue, along with their key executives.

Top Dallas companies by revenue and executives (2025)

#	Company	Revenue	Key executives	Source link
1	Company A	~$120B	Executive 1 (CEO), Executive 2 (CFO)	*Dallas Business Journal*
2	Company B	~$344B	Executive 3 (Chairman & CEO)	*Dallas Business Journal*
3	Company C	~$26B	Executive 4 (CEO), Executive 5 (CFO)	BuiltIn Dallas
4	Company D	~$20B	Executive 6 (CEO), Executive 7 (CFO)	Dallas 500

continued on next page

#	Company	Revenue	Key executives	Source link
5	Company E	~$18.5B	Executive 8 (CEO), Executive 9 (CFO)	Dallas 500
6	Company F	~$1.1B	Executive 10 (Founder & CEO)	CompWorth
7	Company G	~$132.8M	Executive 11 (CEO)	CompWorth

Key insights

- Company A remains Dallas's largest company by revenue, anchoring the telecom sector.
- Company B dominates energy revenues globally.
- Company C continues to be a major employer and revenue driver in aviation.
- Company D highlights Dallas's strength in healthcare services and hospital networks.
- Company E is a global leader in semiconductors, reinforcing Dallas's tech presence.
- Emerging firms like Company F and Company G show Dallas's growing diversity in real estate and insurance.

AI can also be useful in quickly analyzing specific industry trends.

Box 7. Regional business trends

Summarizing five top business trends in Dallas, Texas

Copilot: Creating from within Word and formatting for Word

Prompt: City-wide business trends

Follow-up prompt: **Who are the top ten clients that are affected by these trends?**

Top five current trends shaping the Dallas business landscape

Trend	Description
Technology and innovation growth	Dallas is experiencing rapid growth in technology start-ups and innovation hubs, attracting investments and talent in areas like AI, software development, and fintech.
Real estate expansion	Commercial and residential real estate markets remain strong, with ongoing development projects and increased demand for office spaces and housing.
Healthcare industry advancement	The healthcare sector is expanding, with major hospitals and medical research centers investing in new facilities and telemedicine services.
Diversity and inclusion Initiatives	Businesses are prioritizing diversity, equity, and inclusion, implementing programs to support a more inclusive workforce and leadership.
Sustainable business practices	Many Dallas companies are investing in sustainability, adopting eco-friendly practices and green technologies to reduce their environmental footprint.

Finding market data can be a chore using standard search engines, and even with subscription services. AI can simplify this research.

Box 8. Regional business trends

Summarizing five top business trends in Dallas, Texas, with market data

Copilot: Creating from within Word and formatting for Word

Prompt: Added market data

Dallas's top business trends in 2025 include corporate relocations, tech expansion, real estate growth, healthcare shifts, and investment momentum.

Five top business trends in Dallas (2025)

#	Trend	Market data/insights
1	Corporate relocations & HQ growth	Dallas–Fort Worth ranked #1 in the US for HQ relocations, attracting 100 new headquarters between 2018 and 2024. In 2024 alone, 96 companies announced HQ moves, up from 18 in 2023.
2	Startup & tech ecosystem expansion	Dallas added 14,000 tech jobs in 2025, part of 20,000+ in North Texas. STEM wages grew 33 percent, and start-ups raised $1B+ in capital. Major firms like SearchTech Co., Social Platforms Co., and Enterprise Cloud Co. expanded into the region.
3	Real estate & construction boom	DFW authorized 71,788 new housing units in 2024, leading the nation. Industrial vacancy continues to decline, and Dallas is predicted to be the hottest US real estate market in 2025.

continued on next page

#	Trend	Market data/insights
4	**Healthcare industry shifts**	Dallas hospitals saw 33 percent net income growth in 2025. Medicaid HMO enrollment dropped 24 percent, while Medicare Advantage covers 60 percent of Texans. Ambulatory centers and micro-hospitals are expanding.
5	**Finance & investment momentum**	Dallas is described as a "powerhouse for growth & investment" in 2025, driven by corporate relocations and population growth. The Dallas Fed forecasts 1.5–1.7 percent job growth despite national slowdowns.

Key takeaways

- Corporate relocations remain Dallas's strongest driver, with Fortune 500 firms moving HQs for tax and infrastructure advantages.
- The tech ecosystem is booming, fueled by venture capital, job creation, and expansions from global tech giants.
- Real estate and construction are surging, with Dallas leading the nation in housing development and industrial demand.
- Healthcare profitability is rising despite Medicaid cuts, with new care models reshaping delivery.
- Finance and investment trends show Dallas outperforming peers, attracting capital and sustaining growth.

A good SWOT analysis can take a minimum of two to three hours to research and analyze for a human. AI can reduce this time to minutes.

Box 9. SWOT analysis

Creating a SWOT analysis of A&D in 2025

Copilot: Creating from within Word and formatting for Word

Second prompt: Not necessary

Assessing the strengths, weaknesses, opportunities, and threats of A&D

Introduction
A&D, one of the world's leading telecommunications companies, continues to play a pivotal role in shaping the communications landscape in 2025. This SWOT analysis examines A&D's internal strengths and weaknesses, as well as external opportunities and threats, to provide a comprehensive overview of its strategic position for the year.

Strengths

- Extensive network infrastructure: A&D boasts one of the largest and most advanced telecommunications networks in the United States, offering reliable wireless, broadband, and fiber-optic services to millions of customers.
- Strong brand recognition and customer base: With over a century of operation, A&D is a household name with a loyal and diverse customer base spanning consumers, businesses, and government entities.
- Innovation in 5G and fiber: The company has made significant investments in 5G wireless technology and fiber-optic broadband, enhancing service speed, coverage, and quality across urban and rural markets.
- Robust financial position: A&D's scale and diversified revenue streams from wireless, broadband, and business services provide financial stability and the ability to invest in growth initiatives.
- Strategic partnerships: Collaborations with technology, media, and content providers have expanded A&D's service offerings and helped drive customer engagement.

Weaknesses

- High debt levels: Past acquisitions and infrastructure investments have contributed to a substantial debt burden, which could limit financial flexibility and increase vulnerability to interest rate changes.
- Complex business structure: The company's broad portfolio and history of mergers and divestitures can create operational complexities and integration challenges.
- Customer service concerns: A&D has faced criticism over customer service, including issues with billing, support, and network reliability, which may impact customer satisfaction and retention.
- Legacy systems: Maintaining older technologies alongside new infrastructure can increase operational costs and slow the pace of modernization.

Opportunities

- Expansion of 5G and IoT: Continued rollout of 5G networks and growth in Internet of Things (IoT) applications offer avenues for new revenue streams in smart cities, connected vehicles, and industrial automation.
- Fiber broadband growth: Increasing demand for high-speed internet, especially for remote work and streaming services, creates opportunities to expand fiber-optic offerings to underserved areas.
- Business and enterprise solutions: The rise of cloud computing, cybersecurity, and digital transformation among businesses positions A&D to offer advanced enterprise services.
- Strategic divestitures and streamlining: Focusing on core telecommunications services and divesting non-core assets may improve efficiency and profitability.
- Sustainability initiatives: Investing in green technologies and energy-efficient infrastructure can enhance A&D's reputation and attract environmentally conscious customers and investors.

Threats

- Intense competition: Major competitors such as V, T, and emerging technology companies continue to challenge A&D's market share with aggressive pricing and innovative services.
- Regulatory and legal risks: The telecommunications sector is subject

to evolving regulations, privacy laws, and potential antitrust actions that could impact operations and profitability.

- Technological disruption: Rapid advancements in technology, such as alternative wireless solutions or satellite internet providers, may disrupt traditional business models.
- Cord-cutting trends: The ongoing shift away from traditional cable and satellite TV towards streaming platforms can erode revenue from legacy media services.
- Cybersecurity threats: Increasing frequency and sophistication of cyberattacks pose significant risks to customer data, network integrity, and brand trust.

Conclusion

In 2025, A&D stands as a telecommunications leader with considerable strengths in infrastructure, innovation, and market presence. However, it faces notable challenges, including high debt, customer service issues, and fierce competition. By leveraging opportunities in 5G, fiber, and enterprise solutions while addressing its weaknesses and external threats, A&D can continue to adapt and thrive in a rapidly evolving industry.

Box 10. Competitive landscape

Surveying the competitive landscape in the Rainport market

Copilot: Creating from within Word and formatting for Word

Prompt: What are the top ten law firms by revenue in the Rainport market?

The top ten law firms in the Rainport market by revenue are dominated by large regional and national players with strong local offices. These firms are ranked by gross revenue and attorney headcount.

Top 10 law firms in Rainport by revenue (2025)

#	Law firm	Estimated revenue/size	Key notes
1	C&D LLP	~$1.2B revenue; ~1,200 lawyers	Rainport's largest firm, strong in corporate, IP, and litigation.
2	E&F LLP	~$800M revenue; ~600 lawyers	Nationally recognized, HQ in Rainport, strong in media & healthcare law.
3	G&H LLP (Rainport office)	~$1.2B global revenue; ~1,700 lawyers	Major international firm, Rainport office. Strong in corporate and litigation.
4	I&J PC	~$150M revenue; ~200 lawyers	Regional powerhouse with focus on business, litigation, and real estate.
5	K&L LLP (Rainport office)	~$300M revenue; ~350 lawyers	Strong in energy, natural resources, and environmental law.
6	M&N PLLC	~$100M revenue; ~120 lawyers	Longstanding Rainport firm with healthcare and municipal specialties.

continued on next page

#	Law firm	Estimated revenue/size	Key notes
7	O&P (Rainport office)	~$200M revenue; ~170 lawyers	Focus on technology, healthcare, and natural resources.
8	Q&R PC	~$90M revenue; ~100 lawyers	Known for public policy, media and municipal law.
9	S&T LLP	~$70M revenue; ~90 lawyers	Rainport presence, strong in litigation and business law.
10	U&V LLP	~$60M revenue; ~80 lawyers	Focus on banking, real estate, and maritime law.

Key insights

- C&D and E&F are the clear leaders, both headquartered in Rainport and consistently ranking among the largest US firms.
- G&H maintains a major Rainport presence, although its revenue is calculated globally.
- Regional firms like I&J, M&N, and Q&R remain influential in the local market.
- Industry specialization (tech, healthcare, energy, municipal law) drives much of the differentiation among these firms.

Sources: Puget Sound Business Journal/The Business Journals/Am Law 100 Rankings 2025/Wikipedia: Largest law firms by revenue

Copilot prompt

Would you like me to break down these firms by their Rainport-specific attorney headcount and practice strength so you can see which industries they dominate locally?

Notice that some of the Copilot reports have suggested prompts for more focused research, including timelines, detailed profiles, and further analysis. Keep in mind that there is no perfect prompt, so you may have to try several before getting what you really want. Always check the facts, cited data, quotes, or cases before submitting them to the requestor to guard against hallucinations. Additionally, note that the cite source may not be a hallucination, but the interpretation and the underlying data may be.

From search to strategy: what comes next

AI is here to stay, improving the way researchers approach problems, but the onus is still on the researcher to perform their due diligence on the results.

The promise of AI accessing both the internal and external knowledge resources is multi-layered:

- The time saved from having to manually compile this information from several resources at once is enormous. The SWOT analysis is an excellent example of this.
- The end user will be able to craft a prompt that will result in both the requested information and the context simultaneously, limiting the amount of information to be sifted through.
- The information compiled by the firm over decades will be easily accessible.
- Getting the answer to a question such as "Can you show me an example of a demurrer I filed before Judge X?" will now be easier than ever.

Enterprise search has come a long way from the initial promise of such systems as Lexis Search Advantage and West KM. Although these systems were light years better than the out-of-the-box search systems, they still required quite a lot of backend maintenance and coding. AI has the potential to streamline the processing and classification process, without the time-intensive maintenance. The holy grail of truly useful enterprise search is finally in our grasp.

Back at my desk and with the help of my AI assistant, I send the reports to the partner, confident that I've checked all the sources in the report synthesized by Copilot. Time to move on to the next urgent request... and purchasing those pointy ears.

Reference

1 See the following for a more detailed exploration of the management of security concerns and implementing AI in a law firm environment: Gediman M, "Managing expectations: practical steps to achieve successful AI implementation" in: Ramadan F (ed), *AI and the Legal Profession: Transforming the Future of Law*, 2nd ed, London: Globe Law and Business; 2025.

Chapter 5: From copilots to agents: the next KM frontier

By Chad Ergun, chief information officer, Womble Bond Dickinson

Introduction: the tectonic shift

The legal industry is approaching a tipping point, as the use of agentic artificial intelligence (AI) transitions from novelty to a part of daily practice. After years of muted technology adoption, we are now witnessing a tectonic shift from traditional AI to generative (genAI) and agentic AI. The move from embedded AI to task-based chat and actionable agents demands a redesign of knowledge flow and sharing. This Darwinist evolution challenges the foundations of knowledge management (KM) in law firms and the future of knowledge workers across professional services.

For many years, the legal sector has been using traditional AI applications that have been embedded into solutions such as contract analysis and eDiscovery systems. With the introduction of genAI, content creation became a major topic in boardrooms, raising many questions and rendering the future of knowledge transfer uncertain. When compared to its predecessors, agentic AI operates using a uniquely different approach. These models remember prior interactions; advance complex goals through connected steps; and, most importantly, refine their performance over time by making adjustments based on the feedback they store. They carry the early signs of a major shift from reactive assistance to AI-driven guidance: for example, an agentic system does not simply respond to a request to draft a merger agreement clause; instead, it keeps track of the full deal history, reviews past interactions, takes the client's strategic goals into consideration, and pulls in patterns from similar transactions that the firm has handled. It operates less like a tool, and more like a junior associate who has been assigned to the matter. However, this associate has perfect memory, unlimited capacity, and the ability to work across multiple matters simultaneously.

Understanding agentic AI in the legal context

Beyond task execution

The distinction between chat-based AI and agentic AI in legal practice is becoming more visible as the AI models demonstrate improvement in certain functions, such as memory retention and reinforced learning. The task-driven large language models (LLMs), which have gained significant traction in recent years, function as sophisticated assistants. They become experts at discrete tasks, such as summarizing depositions, extracting key dates from contracts, or suggesting relevant case law with references. Their operation follows a clear input, process, and output pattern. Each interaction gets handled without extended context retention or cumulative learning, so this makes them effective for single-step tasks; however, they are limited when it comes to adaptive reasoning.

The introduction of agentic AI shutters this cycle fundamentally. These systems monitor matter lifecycles with continuous understanding of the full legal engagement context. When reviewing a document, an agent does not just analyze the text in front of it – it also evaluates the document's role in the larger transaction; its relationship to other agreements; and the strategic goals it serves. This contextual intelligence alters the nature of AI assistance from tactical support to proactive advisory.

The consequences of this approach extend far beyond just productivity gains or time savings. When an agentic system reviews a purchase agreement, it simultaneously tracks how certain provisions have evolved through negotiations; identifies potential conflicts with related documents; pushes modifications based on the firm's precedent database; and anticipates issues that might arise in future phases of the transaction. It maintains this awareness throughout the matter lifecycle, building an increasingly sophisticated understanding of the engagement.

The architecture of legal agents

The technical architecture underlying agentic AI models comprises multiple interconnected and complex components. At its foundation is the context management system, which maintains a dynamic outline of all relevant information about active matters. This isn't just a simple data storage and update process; instead, it is an interactive workflow of organizing, prioritizing, and relating information to create a logical model of legal cases.

The second critical layer is the goal orchestration workflow. Legal work is not based on a single exchange but, rather, requires coordinating multiple activities toward predefined strategic targets. A legal research question becomes a memo; a client email; a clause in a draft; a tracked change during negotiation; and, finally, a precedent for future engagements. A platform that operates across those steps, remembers limitations, and cites from firm-approved precedents reduces non-billable work and increases consistency. More importantly, it creates a continuous learning loop in which outputs that are refined through supervising partners' feedback become part of the agent's memory and are added to the firm's knowledge base.

With the introduction of persistent memory, legal agents' capabilities extend beyond the research and retrieval of simple information. These systems contain multiple memory types: episodic memory for specific interactions and decisions; semantic memory for legal principles and firm standards; and procedural memory for workflow patterns and best practices. This multi-layered memory system enables agents to apply lessons learned from one matter to another, while maintaining appropriate confidentiality requirements.

Within this architecture, the learning mechanism deserves particular attention. While traditional AI systems remain stagnant after deployment, agentic systems continuously refine their capabilities through interactions. When a partner corrects a contract provision suggested by an agent, the system analyzes the correction to understand the underlying principle, updates its knowledge base, and applies it to similar situations in the future. This process creates a cycle in which the agent becomes increasingly aligned with the firm's specific practices and standards. If implemented with an explicit reward signal and policy optimization, this becomes reinforcement learning (RL).

Structural requirements for adoption

Building the human–machine collaboration framework

Most law firms trying to successfully integrate agentic AI realize that it is not just a large-scale technology project; instead, it requires a fundamental redesign of how lawyers and systems collaborate. The lawyer–technology–process framework must account for technical integration, professional relationships, ethical responsibilities, and the long-standing cultural habits that define legal practice. This tiered oversight model represents a critical structural innovation. Some agent activities carry less risk or do not require identical levels of human supervision, so a well-designed framework distinguishes between different categories of agent authority. For example, read-only research agents might operate with minimal oversight, free to explore case law databases and analyze documents without direct supervision. These agents pose minimal risk, as they cannot change work product or communicate with external parties. On the other hand, editing agents possess the ability to draft documents and suggest modifications, but require human approval before implementing changes. Some examples of this category might include agents that prepare first drafts of routine agreements, generate legal memoranda, or compile discovery responses. While these agents can create content, their output passes through human review before becoming an official work product. At the highest tier, execution agents possess the authority to take certain actions autonomously within strictly defined parameters. These might include agents that automatically file routine court documents, manage calendaring systems, or send standardized client communications. The parameters governing these agents require careful definition and continuous monitoring to ensure appropriate operation.

Trust structures and accountability protocols (trust, but verify)

Since the introduction of agentic AI, one of the greatest challenges in legal practice is the development of robust trust structures that are verifiable. This multi-tier model covers trust in technology's capability, reliability, and its alignment with professional standards, and that accountability can be properly assigned when issues arise. This approach requires comprehensive audit trails that document every decision and action taken by agentic systems. These trails must be more than simple logs, as they need to provide defensible explanations of the agent's reasoning process. When an agent recommends a particular legal strategy, the audit trail should show why and what precedents were considered, what factors were weighted, and what alternatives were evaluated and rejected. This should be similar to a cross-examination, providing an interface where the agent can be interviewed or directly questioned about its decision points, which could represent another important safeguard to allow human reviewers to check its integrity.

Professional trust requires alignment with ethical obligations and practice standards. Agentic systems must reflect ethical, confidentiality, and conflict rules, and they must explain context with nuance. An agent should flag situations where human judgment is required and add it to the audit trail.

The safety protocols must specify who is responsible when agents are involved, covering both errors for liability and credit for successful outcomes. Partnership structures and compensation models may need to evolve to account for value created through human–agent collaboration, rather than purely human effort. This shift could also disrupt the traditional billing models and accelerate a decline of traditional hourly models used across much of the professional services industry.

Governance and risk management

From a risk management perspective, implementing agentic AI requires comprehensive governance structures that address both operational and strategic challenges. The real challenge is to strike a healthy balance between innovation and risk management. The efforts to gain efficiency must respect professional standards, ethical duties, and the interests of clients.

The risk assessment framework for agentic systems must address multiple categories of potential exposure: technical, professional, and strategic. Technical risks include system failures, security breaches, and algorithmic biases or hallucinations. Professional risks cover malpractice liability, ethical violations, and reputational damage. Strategic risks involve competitive disadvantages from slow adaptation, compliance pressure from government agencies, and elevated expectations from clients for safety measures.

When compared to other industries, law firms face significant consequences when risk management and governance fail, due to their ethical duties, confidentiality obligations, and the close scrutiny of clients. A well-designed quality assurance program requires new methodologies. The traditional review model assumes a human-generated work product, with quality assurance focusing on content and judgment. However, agent-generated work requires additional validation layers that include checking for hallucinations; verifying source accuracy; and ensuring high relevance. These processes must be efficient enough to preserve the productivity benefits while being sufficiently thorough to maintain quality standards.

The transformation of KM professionals

From librarians to architects

The rise of agentic AI fundamentally transforms the role of traditional KM teams within law firms. The traditional model, in which KM professionals serve primarily as custodians and organizers of collective knowledge content, is becoming obsolete, as AI agents can instantly analyze vast repositories of case law with in-house collection. The next generation of KM professionals must evolve into architects of intelligent agents, designing workflows, protocols, and learning mechanisms that enable effective human–agent collaboration. This new architectural role requires a unique combination of skills: KM professionals must understand the technical capabilities of agentic systems; the principles of data science; and the complex requirements of legal practice. They will act as a conduit between agents and humans, where they add value by taking ownership of decisions that require human judgment.

While focusing on this model, workflow design emerges as a critical skills competency. KM professionals must map existing legal processes, identify components suitable for agent involvement, and redesign workflows to optimize human–agent collaboration. This requires a deep understanding of how legal matter management works through the organization. A workflow that made sense when handled entirely by humans may be inefficient or inappropriate once agents are involved.

This new role requires continuous optimization. As agents operate and learn, KM professionals must monitor their KPIs, identify areas for improvement, and implement refinements. Standard models such as Lean Six Sigma can be applied to assess not just efficiency metrics, but also quality indicators, risk factors, and alignment with strategic goals.

Agent design and behavioral analysis

KM professionals must become skilled in designing agent personas, incorporating detailed specifications of how agents should behave in different situations. These personas go beyond rulesets to include communication style, decision-making frameworks, and escalation triggers. For example, consider the design of an agent supporting contract negotiation. The KM professional must define not just what the agent knows about contract law, but also how it should engage in the negotiation process. Should it adopt an aggressive posture or a collaborative approach? How should it balance between competing interests? When should it escalate to human involvement? These design decisions significantly impact the agent's effectiveness and acceptance by legal professionals while reducing potential errors.

Behavioral analysis represents another crucial competency. KM professionals must continuously monitor agent performance not merely for errors, but also for patterns that might indicate systemic issues, algorithmic biases, or improvement opportunities. This analysis requires a sophisticated understanding of both statistical patterns and legal nuances. An agent that achieves high efficiency metrics might still be problematic if it consistently takes positions that, while legally defensible, do not align with the firm's strategic approach.

The feedback loop between analysis and design becomes critical. Insights from behavior analysis must translate into design improvements, which generate new behaviors requiring analysis. This iterative process demands that KM professionals maintain current knowledge of both technological capabilities and evolving legal practice standards.

Core competencies in the agentic era

In the age of agentic AI, the core competencies required for KM professionals extend far beyond traditional expertise. This emerging skills list includes prompt chaining, context engineering, and iterative training loops. Prompt chaining – the ability to decompose complex legal tasks into sequences of agent interactions – becomes fundamental. This isn't just writing effective prompts, but orchestrating multi-step processes in which each agent task builds on previous results to achieve sophisticated outcomes.

The context engineering concept emerges as perhaps the most sophisticated competency. KM professionals must design systems that provide agents with appropriate context for decision-making without overwhelming them with irrelevant information or the "white noise" of data. This requires a deep understanding of information architecture, relevance assessment, and the specific contextual needs of different legal tasks. Consider a complex M&A transaction involving multiple jurisdictions, regulatory frameworks, and business objectives. The context engineering challenge involves determining what information an agent needs at each stage of the transaction; how that information should be structured; and how the context should evolve as the transaction progresses. Too little context and the agent makes poor decisions; too much, and it becomes paralyzed by complexity.

Another critical competency is iterative training loops. The traditional software normally operates according to fixed algorithms, but agentic AI systems continuously update their memory and adapt. KM professionals must design and manage training processes that improve agent performance while maintaining consistency and reliability. This involves curating the right training data, designing evaluation metrics, and implementing feedback flows to update memory.

Practical applications in legal practice

Knowledge extraction from prior matters

One of the most practical uses of agentic AI is turning a firm's prior matters and experience into usable knowledge. Traditional KM systems could store and index documents, but extracting actionable insights requires significant manual effort. There are human-centric approaches to harvesting, anonymizing, and sharing precedent content using professional support lawyers (PSLs) or resource attorneys. However, these manual options are costly, require ongoing maintenance, and risk becoming outdated. In contrast, agentic AI systems can convert a repository or precedents bank into an active knowledge advisory through knowledge-surfacing agents, with only supervisory human input. For example, let's consider how an agent approaches a new merger transaction for a client. Instead of simply retrieving similar prior deals, it analyzes the entire collection of the firm's M&A experience to identify patterns, extract successful strategies, and recognize potential pitfalls. It analyzes how specific deal structures performed; which negotiation tactics proved effective; and what post-closing issues arose. This model is tailored to the specific characteristics of the current engagement and can be repurposed to improve future transactions. The agent's analysis extends beyond document or email activity review to cover the full lifecycle of prior matters: it examines timelines to understand typical transaction progress; reviews time entries to identify resource requirements; and analyzes correspondence to understand client communication patterns. This comprehensive extraction creates a rich knowledge base that informs every aspect of the new matter.

One of the underestimated benefits of this model is its ability to identify hidden connections and connect the dots. For example, an agent might recognize that a routine provision in a shrink-wrap agreement leads to significant disputes in prior matters, or that a particular negotiation strategy consistently results in better outcomes with certain types of counterparties. While even experienced practitioners can miss such hidden patterns when reviewing past engagements, agents can surface and flag them consistently.

Continuous content analysis during matter lifecycle

Agentic AI is fundamentally changing how legal teams understand and manage their client engagements based on real-time analysis throughout a matter's lifecycle. Rather than periodic reviews or milestone assessments, agents provide ongoing intelligence about matter developments, identifying trends, risks, and opportunities as they emerge.

In commercial litigation practice, agents continuously analyze the growing collection of discovery documents, deposition transcripts, and legal memoranda. They identify evolving themes in witness testimony, track consistency across different sources, and flag potential contradictions or weaknesses. This is not simple keyword-searching or concept clustering, but dynamic case analysis that continuously learns from reinforced training. These types of matter lifecycle agents continuously analyze external factors impacting the matter as they run alongside engagements. They monitor relevant regulatory developments, track similar cases in other jurisdictions, and proactively identify changes that might impact transaction structures. This dynamic scanning ensures that legal teams do not get caught unprepared by external developments and can proactively adjust their strategies.

For transactional practices, continuous analysis covers deal document evolution, negotiation dynamics, and client communications. These agents can track how negotiations shift through versioning of drafts; identify emerging deal-breakers; and recognize when they are stalling. They can proactively alert deal teams when counterparties suggest hidden concerns or when email communication patterns indicate relationship issues.

Building knowledge networks and collective intelligence

Agentic AI enables the creation of sophisticated expertise networks that exceed individual knowledge and experience. These networks, in addition to connecting knowledge workers with relevant expertise, also blend collective intelligence across the organization and make it accessible at the point of need.

The strength of these networks depends on agents that can recognize and map expertise across the firm. By analyzing attorney work products, communication patterns, and matter outcomes, they build a nuanced picture of each professional's capabilities. This goes beyond simple practice area classifications to cover specific skills, industry expertise, and even working style preferences. For lateral hires who bring external expertise into a new organization, manual training of the model can be handled during the onboarding process for successful integration. Throughout a matter lifecycle, agents can identify practitioners with relevant experience, even when the fact patterns differ. An attorney handling a blockchain dispute, for example, might be matched with a colleague whose internet commerce or intellectual property work raises similar legal questions across different technologies.

The collective and reinforced memory feature of these agents transforms how firms leverage their cumulative experience. Instead of knowledge residing in individual files or scattered documents or emails, agents maintain fully accessible records of the firm's collective experience. This includes not just what was done, but why decisions were made, what alternatives were considered, and what lessons were learned.

The mentor agents

Preserving institutional wisdom

One of the most impactful applications of agentic AI is capturing and preserving the wisdom of seasoned practitioners or "rainmakers". These agents do much more than just storing knowledge: they encode judgment patterns, analytical frameworks, and strategic thinking that define top-tier practice. They can be also used to assist with mentoring incoming classes or the orientation of lateral hires.

The development of mentor agents begins with an extensive analysis of the practitioner's work product, including briefs, memos, contracts, and correspondence. However, the agent doesn't simply memorize these documents; it extracts the underlying patterns of thought and decision-making. How does this partner approach risk assessment? What factors do they prioritize in negotiations? How do they build arguments in complex litigation? These patterns, accumulated over decades of practice, become the foundation of the mentor agent's intelligence.

With appropriate consent and governance frameworks, firms can create mentor agents that preserve the unique contributions of retiring partners. These agents don't replace human mentorship but augment it, ensuring that accumulated wisdom remains accessible even as partners leave the firm. A junior associate working on their first hostile takeover can receive guidance that reflects the judgment patterns of the firm's most experienced M&A partners, even if those partners are no longer available for direct consultation.

These mentor agents apply judgment and strategy and adapt their guidance to the specific context. For instance, when advising on negotiation strategy, a mentor agent considers not just the legal issues in hand, but also the business dynamics, client relationship factors, and strategic goals that the original practitioner would have evaluated. This contextual intelligence turns the agent's advice from canned suggestions into practical, situation-specific guidance that reflects how experienced lawyers actually think.

Accelerating professional development

Mentor agents change how lawyers grow in the firm by making mentoring a continuous and personalized process, rather than a series of interactions with their mentors. Traditional mentoring has known limitations: senior lawyers have limited non-billable time, and matching the right mentor with the right mentee is often hit-or-miss. Well-designed mentor agents help to close these gaps while preserving the judgment, relationship, and sponsorship that come from real human mentors. These agents provide on-demand access to collective wisdom, allowing associates to receive guidance precisely when needed. An associate drafting their first merger agreement at midnight doesn't need to wait for the morning to get input on structuring earn-out provisions, as the mentor agent can immediately provide guidance based on the firm's collective experience with similar provisions, explaining not just what to include but why certain approaches work better in specific situations.

The mentor agent model is best adopted with a customized approach. The personalization or learning process starts with analyzing an associate's work product and learning patterns to tailor their guidance to their individual needs. For instance, an associate who consistently struggles with securities law issues might receive more detailed explanations in this area, while another who excels at regulatory analysis might get advanced insights that push their capabilities further.

This framework also creates what-if opportunities by providing safe spaces for learning through trial and error. Associates can test different ideas, explore alternative models, and make mistakes without real-world consequences. The mentor agent can simulate counterparty responses, anticipate objections, and demonstrate the impact of different choices. This experimental learning – traditionally only available through actual practice – becomes accessible in a risk-free environment.

Ensuring continuity and consistency

Mentor agents play a crucial role in maintaining continuity and consistency across organizations, especially as firms face increasing attorney mobility and generational transitions. When senior partners retire or lateral partners join, the firm's accumulated knowledge or "secret sauce" does not have to be lost or diluted. Mentor agents serve as institutional memory, preserving and transferring the firm's unique culture and methods.

This continuity advantage extends to client relationships. Long-term clients value not just outside counsel's capabilities, but the specific approach and judgment of their advisors. During client or attorney transfers, these mentor agents can help to maintain the qualities of a particular relationship and ensure client confidence. A new partner taking over a significant client relationship can leverage mentor agents to understand not just the client's legal history, but also their strategic preferences and habits.

In order to ensure successful transfer, consistency elements need to be built into mentor agents across the organization. While individual judgment and creativity remain essential, agents can make sure that fundamental standards and methods remain consistent. This consistency proves particularly valuable for clients who engage multiple practice groups or offices, ensuring that they receive coherent advice, regardless of which specific attorneys are involved.

The evolution from prompting to designing agents

Task decomposition and context understanding

The move from prompt-based AI to becoming involved in the shaping of how agents behave represents a real change in the ways in which lawyers work with these systems. It requires different ways of thinking and a set of practical skills that go well beyond writing creative prompts. The foundational skill in this agent design phase is task breakdown. Legal practitioners need to focus on analyzing complex legal work not as individual tasks, but as interconnected collection of subtasks, each with specific inputs, outputs, and dependencies. For example, a complex litigation matter is divided into document review, fact analysis, legal research, argument construction, and numerous other components.

However, successful decomposition goes beyond simple categorization to understand how these components interact and impact each other. The hands-on skills required in task decomposition become apparent when considering a routine activity like contract review. Surface-level decomposition might identify tasks like "identify key terms" and "flag unusual provisions." However, effective agent design requires much deeper analysis: what constitutes "unusual" in different contexts? How do provisions interact with each other? What external factors should influence the review? The decomposition workflow needs to capture judgment and strategy that skilled attorneys bring to the task.

Context understanding is another crucial evolution step when compared to simple prompting. When working with task-based AI tools, users provide context through prompts. With agentic systems, designers must create frameworks that enable agents to identify, gather, and appropriately weigh contextual data independently. This requires advanced understanding of what context matters for different legal tasks and how that context should influence agent behavior.

Grounding, auditability, and alignment

A reliable design of effective legal agents must prioritize three critical characteristics: grounding in factual accuracy; auditability of decisions and outputs; and alignment with firm values and risk tolerance.

The concept of grounding requires that agents base their outputs on verifiable information, rather than unverified data. This becomes particularly important in legal contexts, in which accuracy is crucial and hallucination could have serious consequences. The outputs from these agents must be tied to specific sources, firm precedents, or verified facts from matter documents. The grounding process extends beyond simple citation to handle logical reasoning that can be traced and validated.

Auditability requires that every significant decision or recommendation made by an agent can be examined and understood. This isn't simply logging activities; it requires creating interpretable records of reasoning processes. When an agent recommends a particular legal strategy, the audit trail should reveal not just the recommendation but the analysis that led to it: what factors were considered; how they were weighted; what alternatives were evaluated; and why the recommended approach was selected.

In order to align with firm values and risk tolerance, advanced calibration of agent behavior is required. Disparate firms have different appetites for risk, varying approaches to client service, and distinct cultural values. For example, an agent designed for a litigation boutique will behave differently from one designed for a conservative corporate firm or in-house counsel.

Transforming static knowledge into living systems

The ultimate achievement in agent design lies in transforming static knowledge repositories into living, adaptive systems that learn and evolve with the organization. Regardless of how well they are organized, traditional KM systems remain fundamentally static. Documents in KM libraries might be updated regularly, but the system itself does not self-learn or adapt to changing needs. Agentic AI systems fundamentally fix and improve this outdated model. By utilizing persistent memory, living knowledge systems refine their understanding over time based on interaction patterns, outcome feedback, and environmental changes. As matters advance, attorneys routinely modify agent-generated drafts in specific ways. The system learns from these adaptations and updates its models to align with preferred approaches. This learning loopback operates at individual preferences, practice-group standards, and firm-wide patterns.

The adaptive capability extends to recognizing and responding to changes in the legal environment. When new regulations emerge or court decisions shift legal landscapes, living knowledge systems don't wait for manual updates: they identify these changes, assess their implications, and adjust their guidance accordingly. This environmental responsiveness ensures that the knowledge system remains current and relevant, without constant human maintenance.

The evolution from static to living systems also includes the development of emergent intelligence. As agents interact with different matters, practitioners, and situations, they develop insights that weren't initially programmed. They might identify unseen correlations between unrelated elements; recognize patterns; or discover optimal strategies through experience, rather than instruction.

Critical competencies in the new era

People skills over AI skills

It sounds counterintuitive, but the rise of agentic AI actually makes human skills the defining factor for success. Knowing what tools can do is necessary, but it is not enough by itself. The real value is in translating complex processes into clear system instructions; applying judgment where technology cannot; and guiding people through the transition to working with agents.

This shift mostly impacts firm culture and the approach to change management. A successful implementation requires managing cultural change as attorneys adapt to working with AI agents. This involves addressing anxiety over replacement; building confidence in new workflows; and helping them to discover how agents can enhance – rather than diminish – their professional roles. These are fundamentally cultural challenges, not technological problems.

Communication skills become even more critical when agents are involved in legal work. Attorneys must be able to explain to their clients not just what agents are doing, but why their involvement adds value. They must keep the balance between leveraging AI efficiency and maintaining the personal relationship that clients expect from their outside counsel. This can be done with a well-crafted communication plan that builds trust while acknowledging the impact of technology.

For KM professionals, this transition reshapes their role from custodians of static information into architects of dynamic design. Instead of concentrating primarily on content curation and analysis, KM leaders are asked to configure feedback loops, improve agent engagements, and coach lawyers on how to achieve reliable outcomes. These necessary skills again highlight the importance of investing in people skills, culture and change management, and communication competency.

Understanding context, constraints, and intent

The sophisticated deployment of agentic AI demands an in-depth understanding of the context in which legal work occurs; the constraints that bound acceptable solutions; and the often-unstated intent behind legal objectives. These understandings represent distinctly human capabilities that become more (not less) important as AI capabilities expand.

Context in legal practice incorporates business relationships, industry dynamics, regulatory environments, and many other factors that influence legal strategy. Effective agent deployment requires professionals who can identify relevant context and translate it into parameters that agents can understand and act upon. This translation requires both broad knowledge and sophisticated judgment.

Constraints in legal work often prove subtle and multifaceted. Budget constraints are straightforward, but what about relationship constraints that preclude certain aggressive tactics or reputational constraints that make some legally valid strategies inadvisable? Understanding and articulating these constraints requires a deep expertise of the broader implications of legal actions.

Intent often remains unspoken in client engagements. For instance, a client might request a contract review, but their real intent might be to strengthen a business relationship, establish precedent for future deals, or signal strength to competitors. Recognizing and responding to this underlying intent requires emotional intelligence, business expertise, and strategic thinking, which remain distinctly human capabilities.

Bridging human expertise and machine precision

In practice, the real skill in working with agentic AI is knowing how to combine human judgment with machine precision so that they reinforce – rather than compete – with each other. Getting this balance right starts with recognizing what makes human expertise unique. Human expertise brings judgment, creativity, and in-depth understanding that is beyond current AI capabilities. Humans excel at recognizing when situations require unique approaches; when precedent should be challenged; and when seemingly optimal solutions might conceal hidden issues. Human expertise also encompasses the emotional intelligence necessary for client relationships, negotiation dynamics, and team leadership – in other words, the "gut feeling" that is cited by many seasoned practitioners.

In contrast, machine precision offers consistency, comprehensiveness, and computational power that surpasses human abilities. Machines can analyze vast document sets without fatigue; identify patterns across thousands of matters; and maintain perfect consistency in applying defined criteria. They can perform complex calculations instantly and remember every detail of every interaction perfectly.

The bridge between these capabilities requires professionals who understand both domains deeply enough to design effective collaborations. This might involve structuring workflows where machines perform initial analysis and humans provide strategic direction, or creating feedback loops where human corrections train machines while machine analysis informs human decisions. The specific structures matter less than the ability to recognize opportunities for synergy and design systems that realize them.

This emerging transformation fundamentally redefines the role of KM professionals, evolving them from information curators to AI orchestrators. Where KM teams once focused on capturing, organizing, and distributing static knowledge assets, they now design dynamic AI systems, establish grounding protocols, and govern the continuous learning loops between human experts and machine agents. Their responsibilities expand to include prompt engineering, agent behavior monitoring, quality assurance of AI outputs, and the critical task of ensuring that automated systems remain aligned with firm standards and ethical guidelines. Modern KM professionals must simultaneously serve as technologists who understand AI capabilities; educators who train both humans and machines; and guardians who ensure that the pursuit of efficiency never compromises accuracy or professional judgment.

Conclusions: delivering trusted outcomes in the agentic era

Let's start with the end in mind. Ultimately, clients are looking for three basic assurances from their outside counsel: a predictable outcome, timeline, and cost. Historically, firms could only offer educated estimates based on past experience and professional judgment. Agentic AI transforms these uncertainties into measurable probabilities. By analyzing patterns across thousands of similar matters, AI agents can identify the variables that drive success, duration, and expense. This enables relationship partners to provide clients with confidence levels backed by data, not just intuition.

Delivering on that promise requires a fundamental shift in how law firms operate. We are evolving beyond reactive, prompt-based AI interactions towards agentic collaborators that work alongside legal teams. This transition elevates KM from a support function to a strategic entity. KM professionals are no longer just librarians or custodians of document repositories; they are becoming the firm's AI enablers and architects. They orchestrate how agents access matter data, interact with institutional knowledge, and integrate into existing workflows. Most critically, they ensure that these systems augment – rather than replace – human judgment, training lawyers to collaborate effectively with AI while maintaining client privacy.

The human benefits of this transformation extend far beyond efficiency gains or cost reductions. Consider how mentor agents democratize access to expertise, ensuring that junior associates receive high-quality guidance regardless of their location, timing, or partner availability. These agents preserve collective knowledge during generational transitions, while freeing senior partners to focus on creative strategy that demands their deep expertise. The three client promises of outcome, timeline, and cost become more achievable, because AI handles the predictable elements, allowing humans to focus on the exceptional ones.

We are now facing a classic innovator's dilemma. Conventional wisdom often suggests waiting for technology to stabilize and letting others make the mistakes first. However, in the context of AI, waiting is the riskier strategy. Firms that move forward now, despite the unknown, are positioning themselves to set industry standards and brand name recognition. The firms building these capabilities today aren't just adopting tools, but building "institutional muscle memory" that cannot be bought off the shelf later. The next generation of legal practice will belong to firms that choose to design the future, rather than wait for it.

Chapter 6:

From resistance to results: gaining organizational and partner support for AI-augmented legal KM

By Hélène Russell, knowledge and learning specialist, TheKnowledgeBusiness

Why KM must lead AI change

At this watershed moment, law firms face new challenges as they integrate artificial intelligence (AI) – particularly generative AI and agentic AI – into their operations. Knowledge management (KM) professionals play a vital role in leading and guiding these efforts: not only do they have the relevant understanding and experience of information and KM fundamentals – such as the importance of data cleansing, knowledge governance, and taxonomies – but they also tend to have extensive experience in strategic communication, change management, and leading projects that require cultural change across a variety of support lines, as well as amongst practitioners.

Much of the legal sector tends towards a traditional stance, with a resistance to change and a hesitancy to experiment with service delivery options and risk failure. This has led to some firms experiencing reluctance from practitioners to explore AI's full potential, owing to its current lack of faultlessness. However, the 2025 survey[1] from the American Productivity and Quality Centre (APQC) into KM priorities and trends noted that 44 percent of respondents (cross-sector knowledge managers) reported that AI was useful for creating new artifacts and content; 39 percent thought AI was useful for recommending content or knowledge assets; 31 percent reported that AI was useful for intelligent search; and 23 percent reported that AI could be useful to identify and surface expertise inside organizations.

Leadership by KM professionals will be the essential ingredient that the legal profession cannot afford to ignore. From their existing experiences, law firm knowledge managers are well-aware that culture is changed one person and one step at a time, and this chapter aims to support those professionals throughout the many steps required to implement and embed the changes necessary to ensure that these AI projects are long-term successes.

In leading complex projects such as these AI integrations, there are many different frameworks you could use for inspiration and to organize your plans. None of these frameworks are perfect, but I have personally found that having one is useful for reference and in shaping my plans, and that some are more practical for the legal sector than others. In considering AI integrations and culture change around AI products, I suggest that you are aware of the following frameworks and that you utilize whichever of these that work best inside your firm's unique culture:

1. Rogers' Diffusion (for segmenting your audience);
2. Rock's SCARF (to address social threats);
3. Lewin/Kotter and/or the Heath brothers' Switch (for overall change management architecture);
4. Nudge theory (for support in system design); and
5. Purpose alignment/Ikigai, and/or Deci/Ryan's self-determination theory (for influencing and persuasion on an individual level).

Why lawyers resist change

One of the hardest aspects of AI project delivery is the need to influence behavior change when many tools are not yet at a level of accuracy that lawyers are comfortable with. Unfortunately, to gain competitive advantage, firms need lawyers to start changing behaviors now, in order to be ready to take advantage once the tools are perfected.

While current research has not yet identified whether certain personality types are drawn to the law or whether the learning and practice of law affects personality in particular ways, the root cause is unimportant for those working with lawyers. Whether the lawyer personality is formed by nature or nurture, legal practitioners tend to have a strong preference for autonomy; they are also likely to be cynical, perfectionist introverts who value thinking, learning, and fairness.[2]

While some lawyers were initially attracted to the potential innovations offered by AI tools and have been enthusiastic about them in theory, many are now struggling with the realities of changing their ways of working as a result. It is a difficult task for knowledge managers to support them in these changes.

Start with segments: Rogers' Diffusion of Innovation

For larger AI projects, it will usually be useful at the outset to segment your users into groups according to their experience and enthusiasm for the new tools. Rogers' Diffusion of Innovation[3] theory can help to identify adopter categories, so that you can target your efforts strategically:

- Innovators embrace new technology enthusiastically and are willing to take risks. Target them first to build your champion network and create early success stories.
- Early adopters are respected voices within the firm. Leverage their credibility to influence colleagues and accelerate broader adoption.
- The early majority adopt once peers have demonstrated clear value. They will follow as innovators and early adopters establish new working practices.
- The late majority require substantial proof before changing workflows. Provide both quantitative evidence and qualitative success stories to address their skepticism.
- Laggards strongly prefer traditional methods. Allocate minimal resources to this group until later implementation phases, when firm-wide adoption is well-established.

Reducing threat responses: SCARF

The acronym "SCARF" was coined by Dr David Rock[4] in the 2000s to describe five key motivators of human social behavior: status, certainty, autonomy, relatedness, and fairness. Change challenges the status quo, introducing uncertainty, disrupting relationships, and creating perceptions of lack of control, all of which triggers a threat response. When AI projects require change in law firms, lawyers can experience fear across all these domains at the potential of losing knowledge, power, status, and comfort. Additionally, given their high levels of education and strong leadership traits (whatever their position in the firm's hierarchy), they often firmly believe in their ability to take their practice elsewhere, which gives them the confidence to push back on change.

However, knowledge managers have always worked within these confines on complex knowledge projects. Although transformation in relation to AI projects may arguably be more complex than other forms of change, knowledge managers are uniquely experienced in these types of change management projects.

Rock's SCARF framework is useful for leaders managing change, as it provides a checklist for understanding why people resist change and how to minimize the threat response by addressing all five domains during the planned change management process:

- **Status:** Frame AI as enhancing expertise and freeing lawyers for more complex, strategic, and profitable work. Recognize and celebrate early adopters and/or create new status markers around AI proficiency.

- **Certainty:** Provide pilot programs and roadmaps with timelines for the changes and concrete examples of how the tools will work in practice, and offer structured training with clear, quick reference guides.
- **Autonomy:** Involve lawyers in tool selection and implementation decisions and, where possible, use opt-in pilot programs and frame changes as expanding options, rather than replacing preferred methods.
- **Relatedness:** Create communities of practice around AI adoption, share stories of successful use of the new tools, and emphasize the collective benefits of AI usage.
- **Fairness:** Apply consistent expectations across groups, address concerns about billing requirements transparently, and give everyone a voice for feedback.

If you can, try to address multiple SCARF domains simultaneously for maximum efficiency, such as a lawyer advisory group (autonomy and fairness) that publicly recognizes pilot participants (status) while providing clear implementation phases (certainty) and creating peer support networks (relatedness).

Change models that work in law firms

Change management might have been a topic of study and discussion for decades, but it continues to be a challenge for most knowledge professionals; in fact, in APQC's recent survey, change management was one of the top three topics knowledge managers wanted to learn more about in 2026.

Lewin and Kotter: structured change

Kurt Lewin's three-step change management framework[5] – although originally developed for broader organizational transformation – can be particularly beneficial for law firm leaders seeking to implement changes related to AI. The framework focuses on creating a climate for change (unfreezing from the old way of working), engaging and enabling the organization to change, and then implementing and sustaining change (refreezing in the new way of working). It provides a structured approach that helps leaders to navigate the complexities of technological adoption.

For law firms, where tradition often dominates, the first step – in which leaders create a "burning platform" from which all workers must jump – is the most vital. Leaders can use this phase to explain the pressing need for AI integration, whether that is to improve efficiency, meet client expectations, or stay competitive within the legal landscape as it transforms. Historically, managers have tried to create their "burning platform" by painting such a gloomy picture of life without the change that employees can't help but leap off the platform and change ("If we don't do X, we can't compete, and you will all be out of work"). However, more recent research[6] suggests that triggering negative emotions in this way only tends to work for quick, simple changes. Those who have worked in KM for a while will know that very few knowledge projects require simple compliance-focused changes, and AI projects are no exception to this. When we need people to solve more ambiguous, large problems and embed new complex changes to the way that they work, leaders need to foster open minds, creativity, and hope, encouraging teams to be interested, to investigate, to get involved, and to learn new things, instilling positive emotions such as pride, joy, and contentment.[7]

Once urgency is established, Kotter's more detailed eight-step framework[8] can guide leaders to form a powerful coalition and develop a clear vision for change. In the context of AI, this might involve assembling a cross-functional team of partners, IT specialists, and legal practitioners who can champion the initiative and address concerns around data security, ethics, and job roles. By empowering employees and removing obstacles, leaders can foster buy-in and reduce resistance. Finally, by anchoring AI-driven changes in the firm's culture and continuing to reinforce the benefits through ongoing communication and training, law firm leaders can ensure that the transition to AI is sustainable.

Switch: motivating real behavior change

Another framework I find useful in legal change management is that of the Heath brothers. In "Switch",[9] the Heaths remind us that, although we all think that we are rational creatures and approach change in an analyze–think–change process, we in fact are far more likely to see–feel–change. When lawyers don't support a change after it has been logically explained to them, this is more likely to be because they don't feel enthused than because they don't understand the reasons underlying the change. Instead of relying purely on data or rational reasoning to facilitate change, the Heaths recommend that we take a holistic approach by:

1. Directing the rider;[10]
2. Motivating the elephant; and
3. Shaping the path for change.

Appealing primarily to a team's "riders" (their logical brain) means that they will lack sufficient motivation to do the hard work needed to change. "Elephants" (their emotional brain) may be lazy, skittish, and prefer quick pay-offs over long term-gains, but they provide the energy and drive to move through the stress of change. Indeed, if the elephant disagrees with the rider, the elephant will win, because self-control is an exhaustible resource (as anyone who has been making decisions all day and then tries to decide what to cook for dinner will know).

Knowledge managers can speak to lawyers' riders by creating a vivid picture of the endpoint of the change in language that practitioners understand, scripting activities and processes in detail, and preventing analysis and debate over the "right choice" once a collaborative choice has been made. Beyond rational explanation, law firm leaders can speak to their lawyers' emotions by sharing stories of successful AI use with tangible benefits ("In six months, finding the right precedent will take 1–2 minutes rather than ten minutes, using our AI-driven search") and addressing fears around job security. Talk to frustration, security, and pride, rather than efficiency and effectiveness. Creating quick wins and celebrating early successes through testimonials can motivate staff and build momentum.

Finally, "shaping the path" involves shrinking the change and changing the situation, rather than just the people, by making the desired behaviors easier and more intuitive than the old behaviors. Embed AI-driven practices into day-to-day operations by adjusting processes, providing training, and removing barriers to adoption, such as outdated workflows or lack of access to necessary technology. Make the old behaviors annoying or difficult to access. Get influential partners on board, and provide social proof and celebration of successes at team meetings and as part of normal conversation.

Lastly, the Heaths remind us that, even when we motivate our elephant with positive emotions, most change projects will inevitably go through a "foggy" period in the middle. Good leaders need to anticipate this sense of failure and frustration and be prepared to coach their teams through it (fostering the "not yet..." learning mindset), to avoid their team's elephants feeling defeated. This is not about accepting poor performance, but coming to terms with the fact that a difficult period is a natural waypost on the journey to a new way of working.

In addition to the change management frameworks proposed by Switch and Lewin and Kotter, it would probably also be useful to utilize the thinking behind Deloitte's transformational intelligence model and gather behavioral data during the change, rather than what stakeholders say they want or intend to do. By monitoring how users are actually reacting to process changes, you can intervene early to correct course effectively and efficiently.

Nudge theory: design for adoption

As the Heaths suggest in the Switch framework, it is far easier to change situations and processes than it is to change people. If we can make the new mode of working much easier than the old one, the change is more likely to stick. One method you can use to support this is nudge theory.[11] Nudge theory came into prominence in the 2000s and aimed to harness widely occurring biases and heuristics to design a "choice architecture" to guide people towards better decisions, without actually restricting their freedom to choose otherwise. Research has shown that people tend to stick with preselected options; choose the path of least resistance and the prominent, attention-grabbing option; and conform to social norms.[12]

One non-legal classic example of nudge theory is the urinal fly at Schiphol Airport, Amsterdam, where cleaning costs were dramatically reduced after small images of flies were etched into urinals, providing users something to aim at, reducing spillage by 80 percent. Another example can be found in opt-out organ donation systems (in which you are automatically registered as an organ donor unless you opt out), which has been demonstrated to improve donation rates to 85–99 percent from the 4–27 percent found in opt-in systems.[13]

Nudge theory has been criticized as manipulative and lacking in efficacy in the long term; however, nudges are meant to complement – not replace – other interventions. Actions here are meant to support your wider change management plan; to help you to "shape the path"; and make it easier and more intuitive than old behaviors.

So, what types of nudges could you put into place? You are aiming to make the use of the new tools easy, obvious, attractive, and social, while preserving professional autonomy and judgment. Can you offer an alternative alongside the traditional option (ie, with an AI search function), rather than require the practitioner to navigate to a new, separate tool? Can you make any tools (ie, meeting summaries) opt-out, rather than opt-in? What can be pre-configured or use one-click activation? Can you use peer modelling in your messaging ("18 partners have used AI on similar contracts")? Whichever approach you choose, ensure that all nudges are transparent; include confidence or uncertainty scores; assure there is clear attribution to AI suggestions; preserve easy opt-out mechanisms and transparency over AI limitations; and, most importantly, iterate based on data (track opt-out rates, A/B test default settings, measure how sustained usage is, and survey lawyers about which nudges feel helpful and which feel intrusive). All of these decisions obviously need to be made in conjunction with your IT security and risk management team. However, where you are confident that you wish to switch usage from one tool to another, these nudges can be useful to make changes easier and more intuitive for practitioners.

Motivating individual behavior change: SDT and the purpose alignment framework

I find two frameworks generally useful for considering how to motivate people in relation to KM:

- Self-determination theory (SDT)[14] helps to explain why people are motivated to act in certain ways and what their psychological needs are.
- The purpose alignment framework (often misnamed as the Japanese concept of Ikigai)[15] elaborates on what creates meaning for individuals and helps them to align their activities with things they find meaningful in their personal context.

However, these frameworks operate within important constraints. Herzberg's insightful quote – "If you want people motivated to do a good job, give them a good job to do"[16] – remains relevant: influence strategies cannot compensate for inadequate fundamental conditions of work, poor tools, insufficient support, or unrealistic expectations. Motivation and influence tactics can amplify implementation of effective AI programs; they cannot remedy fundamentally flawed ones or compensate for burned-out employees. Leaders need to address systemic barriers first and then leverage these frameworks to accelerate adoption.

Intrinsic motivation: self-determination theory

SDT distinguishes between extrinsic motivation (driven by external rewards, such as bonuses, recognition, or penalties) and intrinsic motivation (driven by internal satisfaction, such as purpose or enjoyment). Intrinsic motivation produces more sustainable engagement and behavioral change. It emerges when three fundamental psychological needs are satisfied: autonomy (choice and self-direction); competence (mastery and effectiveness); and relatedness (connection, purpose, and belonging).

For AI adoption in legal practice, this means creating conditions where lawyers feel that they have genuine choice in how they adopt AI; confidence in their ability to use it effectively and enjoyment in learning a new, useful skill; and connection to a community of peers engaged in the same journey. This framework can be useful in creating messaging to encourage adoption and to diagnose which need is unmet: are they resisting because they feel forced (autonomy issue)? Are they expressing frustration or inadequacy (competence issue)? Are they feeling alone or unsupported (relatedness issue)? For example, during launch, your messaging could focus on autonomy: "We've identified several AI opportunities for the firm. Each practice group can decide their adoption approach and timeline. Who wants to join the working group?" You could follow this with a development program based around competence, by offering structured learning paths, plenty of practice opportunities, celebration of progress, and accessible support. Lastly, you could create relatedness by organizing regular gatherings, peer mentoring, sharing successes, and celebrating champions as a collective of innovative practitioners.

The purpose alignment framework

The four purpose dimensions are:

1. Passion: What you love to do;
2. Vocation: What you are good at doing;
3. Mission: What the world needs from you; and
4. Profession: What the world will pay you to do.

The idea of this framework is that most people find fulfilment at the point at which the four dimensions overlap, so that you can motivate individuals to undertake additional work or move outside their comfort zone by offering them work that offers fulfilment in one of the dimensions that they are currently missing. For example, being part of an AI pilot program might not add to someone's profession or vocation, but could offer opportunities to explore their passion (technology and innovation) or their mission (improving service delivery).

Lastly, always keep reward and motivation activities under review and remain acutely aware of unexpected consequences. Lawyers are almost always more intelligent than our systems, so check that you are actually rewarding behaviors and influencing them in the right way, rather than rewarding hiding mistakes.

Communication plans, internal relationship management, and using the "client journey" to influence stakeholders

Communication is always a huge part of any change management strategy and is the primary way that you will move users along the steps of their own journey as a user of new technologies. When thinking about communications plans and influencing users and stakeholders, it can be useful to refer to marketing's "customer journey" and plan to take your own internal customers on a similar journey of influence. Knowledge managers are often required to act as "salespeople", explaining and influencing users to adopt new ways of working for the benefit of their organization. There is no point having the best knowledge database if no one knows about it or understands the ways in which it can improve their practice and remove risk for the firm.

The customer journey comprises awareness, interest, evaluation, trial, adoption, and loyalty. In a similar way, a knowledge manager needs to ensure that stakeholders know what their users need from their KM systems; become cognizant of what KM tools and techniques are available to them; understand how these tools benefit their own practice and the success of the firm; trial the tools; and then adopt these tools, embed these into practice, and share their positive experiences with others.

In designing a successful communication plan for your change, it is commonly recommended to have a brand and a communications lead who is accountable for the plan, and to communicate in a variety of ways (formal/casual tones, with a variety of topical foci looking at different outputs and benefits) using different tools and techniques (short-/long-form, audio/visual/written word), depending on the users.

The success or otherwise of influencing techniques often depends on knowing the character and situation of the user. Personas can be helpful, although the amount of work needed might not be necessary and will depend upon the size of your change. Always remember that face-to-face and one-to-one is the most effective way to influence. Mass mailings might appear more efficient than small group coffee meetings; however, if no one was influenced by your mass mailing, it was wasted time.

Most importantly, start out with the mindset that you will need to tell your story multiple times. A single email or meeting is seldom enough to convey the complexities of an AI project and is unlikely to resonate with all employees to the same extent, given the level of diversity in the modern workplace. Perseverance and repetition are more important attributes than skillful advocacy or salesmanship. KM professionals should leverage a range of channels (emails, newsletters, notices to communities of practice, workshops and presentations, one-on-one conversations) to reinforce key messages and ensure that each team member understands the project's significance. Repeated exposure to consistent messaging helps reinforce commitment, making it easier for teams to internalize the project's value. Of course, to reduce the workload required for this, you can develop standardized packs of slides, articles, and template straplines and paragraphs.

Silence during AI rollouts can create uncertainty, leaving room for speculation and skepticism, with a human bias towards negative assumptions. Transparent, regular updates are crucial, even if the message is simply "work is in progress." KM professionals can support this by facilitating open, honest communication that addresses both what is known and what remains uncertain. By managing expectations and acknowledging unknowns, KM professionals help to build trust, demonstrating that the firm is committed to an informed and transparent approach.

AI projects often come with challenges and setbacks, and how these are communicated can significantly impact morale and trust. It is important to deliver difficult news thoughtfully. KM professionals can guide leaders on the timing and framing of such communications to minimize disruption and maintain confidence in the project's trajectory. Empathetic, transparent communication reassures teams that setbacks are part of the process, not signs of failure.

KM professionals often function as a bridge between distinct groups and are experienced in understanding the unique perspectives within different departments. This means that they are easily able to tailor AI-related messages to resonate with varied audiences. For instance, IT teams may benefit from technical details about AI integrations, while legal practitioners may need insights into how AI will streamline case management. By customizing messages to suit distinct roles, KM professionals ensure that communication is both relevant and accessible.

Through these practical communication strategies, KM professionals enhance transparency and buy-in, helping to mitigate resistance and foster a culture where AI initiatives are seen as collaborative, well-supported ventures.

Conclusions

Legal AI adoption undoubtedly challenges lawyers in ways that align poorly with their professional preferences (high autonomy, skepticism of unproven tools, perfectionist standards) and create predictable resistance. This resistance, however, can be addressed successfully through evidence-based change management. The frameworks discussed (Rogers' Diffusion for segmenting your users; SCARF for understanding social threats; self-determination theory for fostering motivation; and nudge theory for intelligent system design) provide concrete approaches grounded in decades of behavioral research. Success depends on combining multiple approaches: addressing autonomy needs while providing structure; building competence while acknowledging discomfort; leveraging peer influence while respecting individual judgment; and designing systems that guide without coercing. The path to acceptance is neither simple nor identical across firms, and implementation will require adapting these frameworks to your firm's specific culture, practice areas, and readiness level, but it is navigable when you understand the psychology underlying resistance and apply proven strategies to address it.

References

1 American Productivity & Quality Center, *2025 Knowledge Management Priorities and Trends Survey Report*, 23 January 2025. See: https://www.apqc.org/system/files/resource-file/2025-01/K015194_2025 percent20Knowledge percent20Management percent20Priorities percent20and percent20Trends percent20Survey percent20Report.pdf?source_nid=592846.

2 For more information on the lawyer's personality, see the research by Larry Richard, Susan Diacoff, and Elwork and Sells.

3 Rogers EM, *Diffusion of Innovations*, 5th ed, New York City (NY): Free Press; 2003.

4 Rock D, "SCARF: a brain-based model for collaborating with and influencing others", *NeuroLeadership Journal*, 2008, issue 1, pp. 1–9.

5 Lewin K, *Principles of Topological Psychology*, New York City (NY): McGraw-Hill Book Company; 1936.

6 See the work of Cooperrider and Whitney and Barbara Fredrickson, as well as the Heath brothers.

7 For more information on how to create a trusting culture of curiosity and candor, see: Edmondson AC, *The Fearless Organization: Creating Psychological Safety in the Workplace for Learning, Innovation, and Growth*, Hoboken (NJ): John Wiley & Sons, 2018.

8 Kotter JP, *Leading Change*, Boston: Harvard Business School Press, 1996.

9 Heath C and Heath D, *Switch: How to Change Things When Change Is Hard*, New York City (NY): Crown Currency; 2010.

10 This idea of rider and elephant is a reference to the rational and emotional parts, respectively, of our brain, first expressed in this way in: Haidt J, *The Happiness Hypothesis: Finding Modern Truth in Ancient Wisdom*, New York City (NY): Basic Books; 2006.

11 Thaler RH and Sunstein CR, *Nudge: The Final Edition*, New York (NY): Penguin Books; 2021.

12 *Ibid.*

13 *Ibid.*

14 Gagne M and Deci EL, "Self-determination theory and work motivation", *Journal of Organizational Behavior*, 2005, volume 26, issue 4, pp. 331–362.

15 Although there is a Japanese concept of Ikigai, meaning "a reason for living", the famous four-circle Venn diagram is a Western adaptation created by Marc Winn in 2014, drawing on the purpose frameworks created by Andres Zuzunaga.

16 Hertzberg F, "One more time: How do you motivate employees?", *Harvard Business Review*, 1968, volume 46, issue 1, pp. 53–62.

Chapter 7:
Extracting expert knowledge: building knowledge systems for people and AI

By Katya Linossi, co-founder and CEO, Atlas by ClearPeople

The urgency of capturing expertise

For every piece of advice given, transaction completed, and discussion that shapes client strategy, law firms have always run on human expertise. Historically, this approach has depended on the specialized knowledge of individual professionals and repositories of supporting knowledge resources. In 2020, the COVID-19 pandemic introduced significant and unprecedented obstacles to this approach. Firms encountered heightened difficulties in facilitating knowledge transfer among increasingly dispersed and hybrid teams.

This challenge has only increased as client expectations have evolved, and there is a greater emphasis on faster and more transparent service, supported by intelligent tools, data insights, and automation. The advent of artificial intelligence (AI), and particularly generative AI, has intensified the pressure on firms to provide high-quality, well-structured content. There is a clear shift underway: firms now need broader access to their institutional knowledge and must make that knowledge available not only to people, but also to AI tools and platforms.

However, to deliver trusted and precise outcomes, AI tools need context and grounding in authoritative, verified data sources. Without this foundation, even the most advanced models can produce results that appear convincing but lack accuracy, relevance, or professional reliability. Tacit knowledge – the experience-based understanding that individuals carry in their minds and is often difficult to express – cannot be directly consumed or interpreted by AI. Unless firms capture and codify this expertise, it remains invisible to the very tools designed to enhance productivity. Firms face the perennial challenge that a significant portion of valuable knowledge remains tacit, nuanced, and locked inside lawyers' heads. Various authors in KM suggest that the vast majority of organizational knowledge is tacit, often citing estimates up to 80–90 percent.[1,2]

Unlocking this type of personal expertise and experiential knowledge has always been key to innovation, problem-solving, and firm success. However, with AI capabilities embedded in most systems, the urgency of capturing expertise has become imperative. To meet these challenges, firms must strengthen their knowledge foundations by combining validated content, rich context, and human insight. This approach ensures that the wisdom built over decades continues to guide decision-making and drive excellence in an AI-enabled environment.

Knowledge has always been – and remains – a true source of competitive advantage, because it is difficult for competitors to replicate, is inherently unique to each firm, and a powerful driver of long-term value. Capturing and scaling that knowledge is essential to long-term success. It fuels responsible AI, strengthens decision-making, and supports the development of the next generation of lawyers. However, the real value of knowledge lies not only in how well it is captured, but in how easily it can be accessed and applied. Even the most comprehensive content has limited impact if lawyers cannot find the right information at the exact point of need, whether in the middle of a client call, a drafting session, or a strategic discussion. The firms that will lead are those that make expert knowledge both discoverable and usable in the flow of work.

The knowledge management (KM) function sits at the center of this transformation, together with innovation and in partnership with information technology (IT). It defines the processes that translate expertise into reusable guidance, enables automation, and ensures that the firm's knowledge systems remain adaptable, integrated, and future-ready. It is increasingly clear that firms must continuously recognize, create, apply, and refine knowledge within the flow of everyday work and across their work products. This continuous cycle fosters innovation and drives incremental improvement. Kessels refers to this as knowledge productivity – the capacity to transform collective expertise into measurable value.[3]

Knowledge is more than documents

With the wide adoption of AI tools across the legal sector and within most systems, knowledge teams are under increasing pressure to provide high-quality, trusted content that feeds these AI tools. However, at the same time, the way knowledge is being generated has changed dramatically. Lawyers no longer work exclusively within the formal boundaries of a document management system or knowledge banks. They create and refine insights in real time within chats, client portals, or shared workspaces, while needing to aggregate both internal and external sources. They are also increasingly using AI conversational outputs as input to work products, thereby producing dynamic, task-specific collections of drafts, analyses, opinions and, consequently, client deliverables. These informal knowledge fragments often contain the richest, most current knowledge in the firm, yet they sit outside traditional governance frameworks and certainly outside the vicinity of the knowledge function.

This represents both a challenge and an opportunity, opening up a path toward more agile and responsive KM. The KM team's role has already been evolving into that of an orchestrator of dynamic, knowledge-centered ecosystems, but this has now been accelerated, pushing the KM function into creating adaptive, intelligent, and human-centered systems that are essential to achieving true content and knowledge productivity.

Types of knowledge

KM rests on the ability to recognize, capture, and apply different types of knowledge – namely, tacit, explicit, and implicit. Each plays a distinct role in how individuals and firms learn, innovate, and make decisions. In practice, these three types of knowledge are not discrete silos, but parts of a continuum. Tacit knowledge feeds implicit knowledge through action and reflection; implicit knowledge becomes explicit through articulation and documentation. Once codified, explicit knowledge can then be reinterpreted and internalized, turning again into tacit understanding. This cycle was visualized through the integration of explicit, implicit, and tacit categories with declarative and procedural knowledge.[4] Declarative knowledge refers to explicit understanding, or knowing about things, while procedural knowledge relates to tacit understanding, or knowing how to perform tasks.

Rather than distinguishing between explicit, implicit, or tacit knowledge individually, an alternative approach is to classify knowledge into three categories (Figure 1):

1. Formal: This is normally highly curated content.
2. Informal: This is derived from content produced in the ordinary course of business.
3. Tacit: This is knowledge that exists in lawyers' heads.

This chapter focuses exclusively on the capture of informal and tacit knowledge.

Figure 1: Types of firm knowledge and areas of opportunity

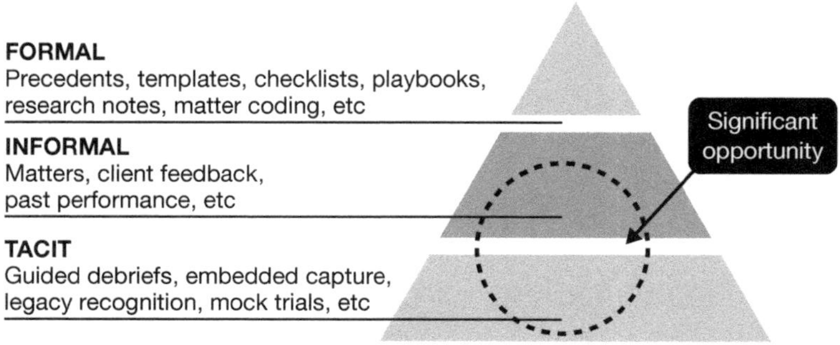

While the capture of formal knowledge continues to be vital, it is recommended that KM leaders make strategic decisions regarding which domains of expertise should be documented and shared more broadly. Areas with significant impact are especially noteworthy, including:

- High-frequency queries from junior lawyers, clients, and legal operations;
- High-risk decisions where guidance mitigates exposure;
- Lessons learned or best practices;
- Novel or evolving areas of law where opinions, precedents, or guidance notes are limited; and
- Insights that showcase the firm's or practice's strengths.

Knowledge capture is the entry point of a continuous knowledge productivity cycle, in which information is gathered, interpreted, shared, and ultimately applied to create value. When capture happens without connection to these subsequent stages, the result is static content. Effective KM depends on the seamless flow between capture, curation, sharing, and application. Andrea Bencsik's concept of the sixth generation of KM reinforces this view, arguing that AI now enables each step in the KM cycle to inform the others in real time.[5] Knowledge capture, in this sense, is inseparable from knowledge discovery and innovation; it both feeds and learns from them. In advanced knowledge ecosystems, information capture is purposeful, contextually relevant, and directly connected to application. This approach fosters a dynamic repository of firm intelligence, where collaboration between individuals and AI supports continuous learning and collective development.

Scaling knowledge

Scalability in KM is all about creating structures, systems, and a culture that can grow and adapt with the firm. A scalable KM ecosystem evolves as new knowledge and new forms of knowledge emerge, enabling capture, curation, and sharing to grow in capability and relevance without adding complexity. True scalability is achieved when knowledge resources expand their usefulness automatically without reliance on manual intervention or administrative overhead. The four key strategies for developing scalable KM resources are:

1. Capture informal, contextual knowledge in the flow of work;
2. Extract tacit knowledge with minimal friction;
3. Democratize knowledge access; and
4. Build collective intelligence.

1. Capture informal, contextual knowledge in the flow of work

Context plays a crucial role in how knowledge is understood, applied, and reused. Knowledge gains real value when it is connected to the circumstances in which it was created, such as the client, matter, jurisdiction, or reasoning behind a decision. Contextual knowledge can, therefore, be defined as the information, understanding, and experience that relates to a particular situation, environment, or set of circumstances.

Contextual knowledge delivers several benefits: it enhances decision-making and creativity, supports effective action, strengthens problem-solving, and enables adaptability in changing situations. To realize these benefits, firms must design systems that embed informal knowledge capture into everyday processes, enrich that knowledge with context, and preserve the reasoning that gives it meaning. Practical ways to capture contextual knowledge include:

- **Storytelling sessions:** Structured storytelling provides an effective way to capture real-world experiences that formal documents often miss. Informal "lunch and learn" sessions, brief video recordings, or written reflections allow lawyers to share lessons learned, explain reasoning, and make contextual knowledge memorable and relatable.
- **Integrate capture into workflow:** Embed lightweight knowledge capture directly into everyday tools such as Microsoft Teams, Outlook, or document management systems. Notes from meetings, client feedback, and informal conversations can all reveal important context about decisions, challenges, and client expectations.

- **Capture reasoning through embedded commentary:** Use client portals or client relationship management (CRM) systems to record the rationale behind actions or recommendations. An example could be: "This approach was chosen because..." These insights make the knowledge richer and more instructive for future matters.
- **Enrich content with metadata:** Metadata is the backbone of contextual knowledge. It defines relationships, identifies contributors, and links content to its purpose. Automated tagging by matter type, client, jurisdiction, or risk profile ensures that knowledge can be located and understood in its proper context.

When context is captured as part of the work itself, informal knowledge becomes more accurate, meaningful, and immediately reusable. Embedding these knowledge productivity practices into the firm's daily workflows transforms knowledge capture from a separate task into a natural outcome of doing the work.

2. Extract tacit knowledge with minimal friction

Unlike explicit knowledge, which is documented in databases, documents, reports, or guidelines, tacit knowledge is difficult to capture, because much of it is instinctive and difficult to communicate. People often don't recognize the value of their own expertise or assume that what they know is obvious or not relevant to others. Additionally, lawyers often do not share insights, due to firm culture, concerns about the accuracy of their input, time constraints, or limited structured opportunities to contribute. Sharing tacit knowledge, therefore, remains difficult, because it is personal, experiential, and often subconscious. Research highlights four main barriers:

- **Language and perception:** Tacit knowledge is largely non-verbal and rooted in personal experience, making it hard to articulate.
- **Time:** Developing and internalizing tacit knowledge takes time and immersion. Lawyers and teams often move too quickly from one matter to the next to reflect and share what they have learned.
- **Value:** Not all forms of tacit knowledge are recognized as valuable. Practical know-how or "rules of thumb" are often overlooked when compared to formal, documented expertise.
- **Distance:** Tacit knowledge relies on interaction and observation, which traditionally has been face-to-face.[6, 7]

Together, these factors explain why tacit knowledge is difficult to capture and share, and why new methods, technologies, and cultural shifts are needed to make the invisible visible.

Extracting expertise necessitates structure, clarity, appropriate incentives, and well-defined expectations. Law firms vary greatly in their approaches; some smaller firms or smaller practice groups within larger firms excel at capturing tacit knowledge. They often thrive because they share a common interest in building expertise; have leaders who prioritize knowledge sharing; and maintain a culture that actively encourages such practices. When leadership demonstrates openness and collaboration, sharing knowledge becomes a symbol of collective strength.

Conventional methods of capturing tacit knowledge

Mentoring and shadowing pair experienced lawyers are commonly used with newer team members to enable knowledge transfer in a natural, interactive way. Structured mentoring programs encourage seasoned professionals to pass on their expertise while building strong professional relationships. This reduces the unconscious nature of tacit knowledge by encouraging active reflection on experiences.

On the other hand, guided debriefs provide structured, knowledge-capture conversations designed to extract insights, lessons, and expert reasoning from lawyers after a significant piece of work, such as a transaction, case, pitch, or client engagement. They go beyond a "post-matter review" by using a consistent, question-led framework that focuses on *how* and *why* decisions were made, not just what happened. A well-designed debrief can turn experience into shared expertise. When integrated into a firm's knowledge workflow and supported by AI tools for summarization and tagging, they become a repeatable, high-value method for converting human judgment into firm intelligence.

Communities of practice (CoPs) bring together lawyers and business professionals with shared interests or expertise to discuss challenges and insights and to formulate best practices. CoPs create an environment where tacit knowledge is exchanged organically through discussions and collaborative problem-solving. Documenting key takeaways from these discussions can help to transition tacit insights into accessible knowledge.

Structured exit interviews provide an opportunity to gather insights from departing lawyers about their experiences, best practices, and lessons learned. These interviews should be designed to elicit valuable information that might not be documented elsewhere, such as project challenges, stakeholder relationships, and unique problem-solving strategies.

Expertise mapping or knowledge about people refers to what is known about individuals and their skills, both within and beyond the firm. This form of knowledge is largely experiential and highly subjective, developed through personal interactions, collaboration, and observation. While much of it resides in relationships and lived experience, elements of this "people knowledge" can be identified, structured, and shared to strengthen collective intelligence. Today, a range of technologies exist to build and maintain detailed lawyer profiles by drawing data from existing internal systems. Each profile typically includes validated data such as spoken languages, jurisdictions of practice, key clients or industry, representative matters, and notable experience highlights. When integrated into intranets, matter portals, or collaboration tools, knowledge about people becomes discoverable and actionable.

The next frontier of knowledge capture

Used responsibly, AI tools and platforms represent a step-change in how tacit knowledge may be captured and transmitted. Rather than relying solely on mentoring or memory, with some types of AI, firms can increasingly leverage technology to remove the barriers to preserve expertise at scale. The challenge for KM leaders is to ensure that what's captured remains trusted, contextual, and aligned with the firm's values.

Some firms are moving away from retrospective "post-matter reviews" toward continuous knowledge capture. Tools embedded in Microsoft 365, collaboration platforms, or document management systems may be used to prompt short, structured reflections at defined milestones during deal execution, client feedback sessions, or matter closure. Questions that might be asked to prompt these reflections include:

- What risks were identified and how were they mitigated?
- What unusual client preferences or commercial pressures shaped the approach, and is it a significant deviation from past practice?
- Which documents, clauses, or workflows should be reused next time?
- Which team members have been involved up to this point, and what were their unique contributions, experiences, and perspectives/insights?
- Why did we or didn't we hit our budget targets?
- Was the client happy with our strategy and our results?

By integrating these micro-debriefs into the flow of work, firms reduce the burden of formal reporting, while dramatically increasing the depth of contextual knowledge collected.

Conventional expertise directories are evolving by leveraging more intelligent systems. These are dynamic systems that connect people, work, and outcomes. Rather than relying on static profiles or manually curated directories, these systems continuously evolve and improve from the firm's activities and outputs, creating a dynamic directory of its collective expertise. In these networks, AI is able to determine lawyers' areas of expertise by examining the work they create, including both client deliverables and thought leadership pieces, as well as the cases they are involved in and the clients or industries they support. This method relies on actual evidence, rather than just self-reported skills, providing a more accurate expertise map. Additionally, recommendation engines can suggest internal experts as lawyers draft, research, or collaborate, surfacing the right colleague or prior work at the exact point of need. For example, a lawyer working on an ESG-related matter might automatically see suggested colleagues who have advised on similar regulatory issues. Finally, analytics can visualize expertise clusters and gaps, showing where strengths are concentrated and where the firm may need to invest in development or training. The evolution from expertise directories to expertise networks also supports AI readiness. By structuring and linking data about people, work, and outcomes, firms create the foundation for intelligent systems that can recommend teams, identify mentors, and power more effective resource allocation. Ultimately, this capability turns "who knows what" into a strategic advantage and enables law firms to mobilize their collective intelligence.

The loss of senior expertise remains a major strategic risk for many firms, and traditional exit interviews or file reviews rarely capture the depth of insight built over decades. Some firms have begun inviting retiring or retired lawyers to record their reflections more informally by email, voice recordings, or short written notes. AI-assisted tools can then analyze, categorize, and store this material by topic, matter type, and theme, transforming unstructured recollections into searchable, reusable insights. While simple, this approach can be remarkably effective. It lowers the barrier to contribution and allows senior lawyers to share wisdom in their own words, while the technology applies structure and context. By analyzing patterns across these documents, emails, and transcripts, firms can build knowledge profiles that reveal how experienced lawyers think and work. Combined with structured debriefs, this creates a living archive of expertise. Some firms use retiring partner dashboards to visualize key matters, themes, and client relationships, prompting targeted knowledge capture before departure. The most forward-looking firms could extend this with AI digital twins that preserve and evolve a partner's expertise long after retirement.

AI digital twins are emerging as a significant area of interest in legal KM. Adapted from engineering and healthcare, they create virtual replicas of systems, processes, or individuals that evolve through continuous data and interaction. A digital twin of a senior partner, for instance, may reflect years of strategy, drafting style, and client communication, allowing the AI to replicate reasoning and provide guidance on new matters. When properly governed, these models act as mentorship tools that support succession planning and knowledge transfer. Twins can also represent legal processes, enabling firms to simulate workflows, test strategies, and optimize resources while ensuring that human oversight remains central. They might also identify essential knowledge held by retiring partners that will be vital for maintaining business continuity.

For KM teams, simulations can also create repositories of collective learning that capture what worked, what did not, and why. Simulation tools use natural language processing, sentiment analysis, and behavioral modelling to simulate mock trials and AI-assisted juries. These systems assess how arguments, witness statements, and evidence may influence perception and bias, giving lawyers data-driven insight to refine courtroom strategy.

The KM team's role may also shift from curation and validation to ensuring that what is surfaced by AI is accurate, relevant, and appropriately classified for reuse. The ethical dimension is that, as with any AI application, replicating human judgment raises ethical and governance questions. Firms must establish clear consent, data provenance, and accountability frameworks. For example, a digital twin should be viewed not as a replica of an individual, but as a structured knowledge asset that is validated, explainable, and bound by the firm's professional standards.

3. Democratize knowledge access

Democratizing knowledge means breaking down the silos and hierarchies that have long restricted the capture and sharing of knowledge, so that every individual in the firm – not just experts or senior leaders – can find, contribute to, and apply knowledge with confidence. In the age of AI and hybrid work, democratization is not just a cultural aspiration, but a competitive necessity. When knowledge is accessible and contextualized for everyone, decision-making accelerates, innovation flourishes, and knowledge becomes a strategic advantage. Strategies for democratizing knowledge include the following.

Embed knowledge in the flow of work
Embedding knowledge in the flow of work means integrating the knowledge lifecycle directly into the tools and moments where lawyers make decisions, draft documents, manage matters, and collaborate with colleagues or clients. It acts as the connective tissue between systems and processes, ensuring that insight is delivered precisely when and where it is needed. In practice, this might mean that, while drafting a share purchase agreement in Microsoft Word, a lawyer automatically sees the firm's "similar" clauses. Another example could be during a client call in Microsoft Teams, in which a partner could easily access a relevant prior matter summary to guide the discussion and anticipate client questions. Embedding knowledge in this way turns it from static reference material into a live resource that supports action. It enables lawyers to apply institutional expertise without leaving their workflow.

Balance openness with governance
Democratization doesn't mean a free-for-all. The challenge for KM leaders is to create an ecosystem where ideas, precedents, and insights can flow freely without compromising data accuracy, confidentiality, compliance, or client trust. Well-governed knowledge systems establish clear rules around these principles:

- Provenance ("where did this come from?");
- Validation ("who approved this?"); and
- Use ("what context is it valid in?").

These elements are equally essential for AI readiness, to ensure that the tools draw only from trusted, verifiable sources. The ideal state is "managed openness" that allows collaboration and contribution, while applying metadata, permissions, and validation layers automatically. It is also important to acknowledge and reward contributions, to emphasize that sharing expertise is highly valued within the firm.

4. Build collective intelligence

Collective intelligence is a kind of wisdom and knowledge that grows out of a group. The concept of collective intelligence states that, when people work together, they form a type of intelligence that simply cannot exist on the individual level. James Surowiecki popularized the concept of the "wisdom of crowds" by demonstrating that the collective judgment of a diverse and independent group can be more accurate than that of any single expert.[8] This depends on three key factors:

- Diversity, where participants bring varied perspectives and experiences;
- Independence, where individuals form opinions free from group influence; and
- Decentralization, where contributors draw on their own local or specialist knowledge.

In a law firm context, this principle applies every time lawyers across practice groups collaborate on a complex transaction; share lessons from litigation outcomes; or co-develop new client solutions. The collective insight of the group often outperforms the expertise of any single contributor.

Today, collective intelligence and AI are increasingly intertwined. AI can process vast amounts of data, detect patterns, and surface insights at remarkable speed, while human intelligence provides the judgment, creativity, and context needed to interpret and apply those insights responsibly. Together, they create a powerful feedback loop: AI amplifies human expertise, and people refine and guide AI to deliver outcomes that are not only faster but smarter and more accurate. For law firms, this combination is compelling, because it enables smarter work. By uniting human and machine intelligence, firms can turn knowledge into a strategic capability that grows stronger with every use.

The KM perspective

For knowledge managers, building collective intelligence means creating an environment in which people and AI continually learn from one another. It requires systems that capture human insight in the flow of work; governance that maintains trust and accuracy; and a culture that values openness and collaboration over ownership. This includes:

- Encouraging open dialogue, structured reflection, and mentoring, which allows knowledge to move laterally through the firm, rather than staying trapped in silos. When lawyers collaborate across practices and geographies, they bring diverse perspectives that improve judgment and innovation. Leadership plays a crucial role here, encouraging curiosity, humility, and the belief that no single lawyer holds all the answers.

- Capturing insights from every interaction across the firm, so that the firm's knowledge grows organically over time.
- Designing the firm's knowledge bases to act as a shared brain, continually learning from each case, process, or procedure. KM teams should be mining patterns across matters, documents, and communication tools to surface connections and insights that would otherwise remain hidden.
- Integrating human judgment with machine analysis, so that feedback loops continually refine content quality and relevance.
- Structuring knowledge for interoperability, ensuring that AI can draw on validated, contextual, and explainable sources.

A firm that masters collective intelligence gains both agility and resilience. It learns faster, adapts more effectively, and delivers greater consistency of advice across teams and offices.

Turning knowledge into scalable outputs

Knowledge is only valuable when it can be reused without losing meaning or intent. Firms typically produce a range of outputs designed to capture and scale knowledge, such as:

- Practice playbooks, which serve as one form of the firm's collective memory. They explain why particular approaches are preferred, how risks are mitigated, and what lessons have been learned from previous matters. The most effective playbooks evolve continuously, integrating new insights from ongoing work and feeding them directly into workflow systems. Increasingly, they can also act as the training corpus for AI assistants, shaping how knowledge is retrieved, interpreted, and applied.
- Precedent collections, which have long formed the backbone of legal KM; however, leading firms are now making them smarter and more dynamic. Clauses, drafting notes, and commentary are interlinked, searchable, and tagged by jurisdiction, client type, and so forth. AI can support this process by comparing versions, identifying anomalies,

and surfacing the rationale behind changes, transforming static precedents into a learning system.

- Learning management systems, which extend this capability into training and development. They enable structured onboarding, targeted upskilling, and the long-term retention of expertise. When linked to playbooks and precedent libraries, they create a continuous learning loop between doing, documenting, and developing.
- Process automation and workflow tools, which turn transactions into repeatable, auditable steps. Automating deal checklists and approval flows reduces risk, improves quality, and frees lawyers to focus on higher-value work. We have seen this approach implemented successfully at firms, where the impact was both immediate and measurable.

Making your valuable outputs readily available

Creating valuable knowledge assets is imperative, but the real advantage comes from making them easy to find, use, and share. The real challenge is locating expertise at the moment of need. Knowledge that sits in folders, emails, or outdated repositories cannot deliver value until it is surfaced in the right place and context.

Designing for discoverability

Knowledge should be deliberately structured to ensure it is easily accessible through the resources commonly utilized by lawyers and legal professionals. This may involve the firm's knowledge repositories, intranet, document management system, and collaboration platforms, as well as AI assistants integrated within Outlook or Word.

The most effective firms are now adopting platforms that combine collaboration, enterprise search, KM, and AI in one seamless environment. These systems provide access to authoritative sources that connect users to validated precedents, playbooks, and expertise without leaving their workflow. AI-powered knowledge assistants enhance this further by recommending subject matter experts, surfacing related insights, and supporting informal knowledge exchange across teams. Crucially, these platforms deliver personalized experience: they surface the most relevant content, contacts, and guidance at the exact moment they are needed. By integrating knowledge directly into the daily workflow, firms transform information retrieval from a time-consuming task into an effortless, contextual experience, ensuring that valuable knowledge is not only captured, but is consistently used to deliver better outcomes.

Context is everything

Making knowledge findable also means making it contextual. Automated tagging, metadata enrichment, and AI-assisted search help ensure that the best precedents, playbooks, or subject matter experts are easily found without unnecessary searching.

Simplifying sharing

Equally important is simplifying the act of sharing. When lawyers can publish and update insights easily through intuitive interfaces with automated or suggested tags, knowledge flows freely across teams and practice groups. Governance remains essential: review cycles, validation workflows, and clear ownership maintain trust in what is reused.

Client collaboration

The same principles extend to client collaboration. As clients demand greater transparency, firms that share curated knowledge securely and collaboratively build deeper relationships. Shared playbooks and AI-enabled Q&A tools within client portals allow clients to engage directly with firm expertise, while the firm maintains oversight and governance. This creates a feedback loop in which client interactions enhance knowledge, strengthening both internal learning and client experience. Knowledge collaboration is likely to play a major role in shaping the future of client relationship management.

Conclusions

The modern law firm stands at a turning point. Expertise has always been its defining strength; however, in an environment shaped by hybrid work, growing client expectations, and the rise of AI, that expertise must now be captured, structured, validated, governed, and shared in new ways. The urgency to capture what people know before it is lost in the pace of delivery or scattered across disconnected systems has never been greater.

Building scalable knowledge resources requires a shift from managing documents to enabling knowledge productivity. This means capturing not only what was done, but why it was done, preserving the reasoning and judgment that transform information into insight. It involves capturing broader knowledge; encouraging contribution, so that knowledge creation becomes part of daily work; and developing collective intelligence that unites human expertise with machine learning. Once captured, knowledge must be transformed into practical, reusable outputs that promote consistent, high-quality work. These resources form a living framework for continuous learning and improvement.

Equally important is making this knowledge easy to find and share. Intranets, intelligent search, AI assistants, and client collaboration portals ensure that trusted information is available in context and in real time. This creates a continuous flow of insight across the firm and with clients, enhancing transparency, efficiency, and innovation.

Ultimately, the firms that will lead in the AI era are those that treat knowledge as a living system that learns and evolves. By capturing expertise, scaling it through technology, and sharing it with purpose, firms turn knowledge into their most sustainable source of competitive advantage.

References

1 Serrat O, "Learning Lessons with Knowledge Audits" in: *Knowledge Solutions*, Singapore: Springer; 2017.

2 McAdam R, Mason B, and McCrory J, "Exploring the dichotomies within the tacit knowledge literature: towards a process of tacit knowing in organizations", *Journal of Knowledge Management*, 2007, volume 11, issue 2, pp. 43–59. https://doi.org/10.1108/13673270710738906.

3 Kessels J, "The knowledge revolution and the knowledge economy: the challenge for HRD" in: Woodall J, Lee M and Stewart J (eds.), *New Frontiers in HRD*, London: Routledge: 2004; pp. 165–179.

4 Nickols F, "The knowledge in knowledge management" in: Cortada JW and Woods JA (eds.), *The Knowledge Management Yearbook 2000–2001*, Oxford: Butterworth-Heinemann; 2000.

5 Bencsik A, "The sixth generation of knowledge management – the headway of artificial intelligence", *Journal of International Studies*, 2021, volume 14, issue 2, pp. 84–101. https://doi.org/10.14254/2071-8330.2021/14-2/6.

6 Nonaka I and Konno N, "The Concept of 'Ba': Building a Foundation for Knowledge Creation", *California Management Review*, 1998, volume 40, issue 3, pp. 40–54. https://doi.org/10.2307/41165942.

7 Smith EA, "Applying knowledge-enabling methods in the classroom and in the workplace", *Journal of Workplace Learning*, 2000, volume 12, issue 6, pp. 236–244.

8 Surowiecki J, *The Wisdom of Crowds: Why the Many Are Smarter Than the Few, and How Collective Wisdom Shapes Business, Economies, Societies, and Nations*, New York (NY): Doubleday; 2004.

Chapter 8: What the client wants: re-engineering legal KM from the outside-in

By Dr Pietro Brambilla, LL.M, senior counsel, Mercedes-Benz Group AG, and legal innovation consultant, Inter Alia

The client has left the building

The most important question in legal knowledge management (KM) is not "What can we show our clients?", but "What can we learn from them?" At Marsh McLennan, the world's largest insurance broker, the legal department saved $9 million in 2024 by bringing legal data management in-house, retrieving information twice as fast as before.[1] At CrowdStrike, use of artificial intelligence (AI) has halved spending on intellectual property advice from external firms and reduced prior art costs by 90 percent.[2] These are not isolated cases; instead, they represent a fundamental shift in how sophisticated corporate legal departments operate and what they expect from law firms. For decades, corporate legal departments were mostly terrible at KM. They had no precedent libraries worth mentioning; no sophisticated search capabilities; and certainly no elegant systems for capturing institutional wisdom. In-house "KM" was a chaotic network of shared drives, email folders, and the tribal knowledge of senior lawyers. Legal departments were dependent on law firms, because they lacked the infrastructure to be anything else. That era is over.

Instead, leading corporate legal departments are building what can be termed their "legal operating system." This is not a single software application; it is an integrated ecosystem that includes matter management, e-billing, entity management, contract lifecycle management (CLM), and eDiscovery platforms that are integrated into the overall enterprise data and technology architecture. The magic – and the value – is not in the individual applications, but in the data that flow between them. Today's sophisticated in-house legal departments have evolved by learning from their business counterparts, implementing the data architectures and analytics capabilities that have become standard in finance, sales, and operations. They deploy (generative) AI (genAI) to conduct legal work; analyze patterns across their entire legal documents; benchmark firm performance in real-time; and make decisions based on predictive analytics. The advent of genAI has not just accelerated this evolution – it has made it imperative.

This chapter provides the "voice of the client", explaining how law firms must pivot from being knowledge custodians to becoming data partners. As in-house legal departments become more sophisticated consumers and builders of AI, their needs have fundamentally shifted. They no longer want access to law firm knowledge; they want law firm data piped into their systems. The future of client-facing KM is not a portal that law firms maintain; it is a data product that clients consume.

The pressure cooker: why speed is becoming non-negotiable

Understanding why this transformation is happening so quickly, and why the stakes are so high, is essential. In-house legal departments operate under relentless pressure from the business. General Stanley McChrystal, reflecting on modern organizational dynamics, emphasized "the need to transform organizations from slow, linear processes to operating at the speed of information and real-time data."[3] This is not military hyperbole, but the daily reality for corporate legal teams operating on two fronts simultaneously: capturing opportunities and managing crises. Uncertainty has become the new normal in modern markets. Global disruptions – from pandemics to inflation to geopolitical disruption – have compressed decision-making windows dramatically.

Speed matters in two critical scenarios. First, when opportunities emerge – whether these are product launches or acquisitions – corporate legal teams operate at transaction speed, not memo speed. The fastest movers outperform competitors, regardless of size. Second, speed is equally essential for crisis response. According to the *Financial Times*, during CrowdStrike's July 2024 outage, when the company's market value dropped 33 percent in days, the legal team needed systems that could instantly surface which contracts contained outage clauses, in which jurisdictions, and with which liability caps.[4] Email chains to law firms and manual document review were simply too slow. Whether capturing opportunity or containing crisis, speed has become table stakes. This pressure has forced a choice: become a bottleneck, or reimagine how we operate.

Alongside speed comes price pressure – a second, equally relentless client demand. Corporate clients have done the math on AI efficiency gains and are demanding that law firms share those benefits. One innovation director at a global firm reported: "We've had conversations with major clients that say to us, 'Look. We expect AI to make things less expensive. You're either gonna figure that out or we're just gonna pay you 20 percent less next year, and you figure it out.'"[5] This is not negotiation – it's an ultimatum. Sophisticated corporate legal departments understand that AI can compress 30–60 percent of legal work by 50–90 percent.[6] They are no longer willing to pay billable hour premiums for work that technology has made dramatically cheaper to produce. Law firms can either lead this transformation with new pricing models, or have it imposed upon them through procurement mandates.

The inside-out trap: how law firms optimized for the wrong client

Examining how the industry arrived at this point is instructive. According to surveys, law firms have invested 70 percent of their AI/KM budget on internal efficiency: automating document review; organizing precedent libraries; and improving knowledge transfer. This makes sense: lawyers spend 25–35 percent of time searching for information; knowledge is siloed in partners' heads; and quality varies across the firm. These investments solve real internal problems.[7]

However, here is the disconnect: the sequential approach – "Fix internal systems first and then deliver better client value" – misunderstands what sophisticated clients actually need. Corporate legal departments do not need law firms to work more efficiently within their walls. Instead, they need law firms to work differently across organizational boundaries. They need integration with our systems, not optimization of yours.

From search tools to AI engines: what changed

To understand why clients are demanding data feeds instead of portals, it helps to step back and examine what genAI systems actually need to function reliably – a technical reality that explains much of the strategic disconnect. There is a dangerous myth in parts of the industry that genAI is a kind of super-associate you can drop into a chaotic knowledge environment and somehow get order and insight as a result. However, these systems do not reason using "the firm's collective wisdom" in the abstract; they assess whatever has been tagged, cleaned, and made machine-readable, such as matter profiles, clause libraries, playbooks, regulatory trackers, and litigation databases. If your tagging, metadata, and document hygiene are weak, the model either hallucinates or drowns the user in irrelevant material. If they are strong, the model looks almost magical to the lawyer, because it finally surfaces the right segment of the right document at the right time, wrapped in a sensible explanation.

This is why the most valuable AI investments many law firms and corporate legal departments could make right now are aggressively unglamorous. Refactoring taxonomies, harmonizing matter types, consolidating practice area silos, and turning unstructured advice into structured data objects will do more for client-facing AI than yet another chatbot pilot. Law firm KM's new job description is simple to state and hard to execute: make the firm's knowledge AI-ready, not just searchable.

What clients actually need: the client mandate

Now, let me be specific about what has changed in client requirements. These are not theoretical demands – these are capabilities that corporate legal departments are already building themselves, demanding in request for proposals (RFP), or creating workarounds for when law firms cannot provide them.

Real-time data feeds, not retrospective reports

Picture your current model, which likely looks something like this:

Matter closes ➡ Lessons learned document created six months later ➡ Knowledge captured in your precedent library ➡ Shared with the client in your quarterly business review

Now consider the corporate reality: legal departments have live dashboards that pull data from ongoing matters across all their law firms. They need to see real-time progress on key milestones, emerging risk indicators, and budget variance – not wait for post-mortem analysis. Why should this matter to you as a KM professional? Because, when corporate teams can see in real-time that three different firms are all spending excessive hours on the same type of regulatory analysis, they can intervene immediately to create efficiency. When law firm knowledge capture happens after the matter closes, that opportunity for optimization is lost.

What legal departments need from law firms is structured data feeds during the matter, not after. This means:

- Standardized tagging of work as it happens (matter type, jurisdiction, risk category, work phase);

- Real-time budget and timeline tracking with structured variance reporting;
- Automated capture of key decisions and milestones with appropriate metadata; and
- Secure application programming interface (API) endpoints that our systems can query without requiring your team to manually prepare reports.

The uncomfortable reality is that, if capturing these data creates friction in law firm workflows, perhaps the workflow is the problem – not the request.

Quantified expertise, not qualitative assurances

Corporate legal leaders have heard the phrase countless times: "We have 20 years of litigation experience in this jurisdiction." However, in an AI-driven procurement process, they need more. Can law firms translate that experience into:

- Predicted case timelines with confidence intervals based on case characteristics?
- Risk factor identification with historical precedent of which issues actually influenced outcomes?
- Success rate analysis for different litigation strategies?
- Quantified impact of specific judicial tendencies, opposing counsel, or venue selection on case outcomes?

The provocative reality is that, if law firm "expertise" cannot be translated into a predictive model or decision-support dataset, corporate procurement teams cannot distinguish it from competitor expertise in their evaluation process. Qualitative narratives and quantitative analysis live in different universes. Corporate legal departments are building internal models that require quantified inputs from external counsel. This represents a fundamental shift from qualitative advice to quantitative decision support:

- **Litigation outcome prediction:** Legal departments need structured data on case characteristics, judicial tendencies, and historical settlement patterns – not just law firm opinions on likely outcomes.
- **Regulatory change impact modeling:** In-house lawyers and compliance specialists need tagged, categorized, and prioritized alerts that feed directly into enterprise compliance management systems – not PDF newsletters.

- **Contract risk scoring:** Corporate counsel need standardized risk assessments with defined metrics and thresholds – not narrative summaries of "key issues."

The phrase "Trust me, I have done this 100 times" no longer suffices when clients can analyze those 100 matters themselves... if law firms will provide the data in usable formats.

Interoperability, not destination portals

Law firm client portals are often beautiful: the search functionality is impressive; the taxonomy is well-designed. However, frankly, corporate legal departments never use them. Here's why: legal departments already have technology stacks that include CLM, matter management, e-billing, compliance platforms, procurement systems, digital front doors, and workflow engines. Law firm portals are login number 47; they do not integrate with anything corporate teams actually use for decision-making. What creates value for clients is not a destination that law firms have built; it is integration with the destinations that clients have already built.

The digital umbilical cord: API-first architecture

The API is the unsung hero of the modern digital economy. It is how weather apps talk to meteorological databases and how travel sites aggregate flights. It needs to be how law firms (also) talk to corporate legal departments.

Consider this scenario: instead of a legal department logging into a law firm portal to check for new developments in data privacy law or sifting through law firm newsletters to find the needle in the haystack, the firm maintains a secure API endpoint. The corporate compliance dashboard pings that API every morning; pulls a structured data feed of the top five global regulatory changes from the last 24 hours; and automatically surfaces them to relevant business units within tools they already use. The value is no longer the knowledge itself, but the seamless, frictionless integration of that knowledge into operational workflow. For law firms, this means:

- Investing in modern data stack infrastructure;
- Structuring internal know-how, case summaries, and regulatory analyses as data objects, not just documents; and
- Offering standardized, secure APIs that allow clients to pull specific data streams they need.

The API-first approach matters because:

- Corporate teams do not want to train their people on law firm interfaces – they want law firm intelligence in their own interfaces;
- They need programmatic access for their AI systems to query law firm knowledge bases;
- They require bidirectional data flow – client matter data should improve law firm models, and law firm intelligence should power client decision systems; and
- Manual processes create "swivel chair" work – corporate staff logging into law firm systems and then copying information into their own systems. This is the opposite of efficiency.

Think of this as legal services as microservices. Corporate legal departments are not asking law firms to become technology companies. They are asking law firms to make their expertise consumable by technology.

Data governance and client confidentiality: the foundation

This bears stating plainly: when you build APIs that pipe data into corporate systems, you are managing client confidential information on the client's terms, not yours. That means role-based access controls (who sees what); encryption standards (AES-256 minimum); data retention policies; and precision about what data are confidential or privileged versus what are not. It also means transparency: if you are using AI to analyze client information, clients need to know it.

This is not novel complexity – it is table stakes. The firms that will command premium pricing from sophisticated clients are those that treat data governance not as compliance overhead, but as foundational architecture. One international law firm decided to build their AI tool in-house, specifically to maintain granular control over client data environments, rather than licensing external AI tools. That was a governance decision not a technology decision. For your KM and IT teams, this translates to concrete work: classifying data assets by privilege status and sensitivity during design phase; implementing role-based access into your API structure; documenting data boundaries in client contracts; and tracking data access via audit logs. Get this right, and it becomes your competitive advantage; however, get it wrong, and this will become your liability. The firms that will struggle are those that treat data governance as an afterthought, bolting on security and compliance after the APIs are already live. That is backwards – you should design for governance from Day 1.

The data moat: why proprietary capabilities trump generic tools

In the age of AI, data have become the most critical competitive resource. The performance, accuracy, and utility of any AI model is fundamentally determined by the quality and uniqueness of the data on which it is trained. This insight fundamentally shifts the competitive landscape for law firms. Corporate legal departments that have built their own AI systems have learned a counterintuitive lesson: the sophistication of the model matters less than the quality and uniqueness of training data. A simple model trained on clean, comprehensive, proprietary data will outperform a sophisticated model trained on public or narrow datasets.

The strategic choice: build or buy?

As the legal AI market matures, law firms face a critical strategic choice. Most firms focus on licensing commercially available, third-party AI platforms to enhance existing workflows. The legal tech market is replete with such tools – Harvey, Legora, Thomson Reuters' CoCounsel, Lexis+ AI – seeing broad adoption for tasks like legal research and document management. This strategy is accessible, relatively quick to implement, and delivers tangible efficiency gains. However, the same is valid for corporate legal departments. Maria Pedrosa Martínez, head of new law and digital at Repsol, reports that the deployment of Harvey AI across the company's 200-person global legal department for tasks such as contract drafting and litigation preparation saved lawyers up to six hours a week.[8] Justine Campbell, National Grid's chief legal officer, sees the main benefit of AI not merely in time savings, but in enabling a fundamental transformation of legal work processes. According to her, such tools can help lawyers collaborate more effectively, share insights across teams, and better identify potential risks.[9] As a result, from the corporate client perspective, there is little to distinguish one firm's use of commercially available AI from another's, because these tools are available to all, including to corporate legal departments. Any efficiency gains are quickly commoditized across the industry. The firm becomes mostly a consumer of technology, not a driver of it.

From licensing to building: the data moat strategy

A smaller but strategically more ambitious group of firms are making significant investments to build proprietary AI capabilities and develop novel, AI-native legal services. This strategy recognizes that the most profound value of AI will not come from performing old tasks faster, but from creating entirely new ways to solve client problems. These firms – call them AI creators – have made a deliberate choice to treat AI not as a feature on their lawyers' laptops, but as a new production line. They are building internal research and development teams staffed with data scientists, AI engineers, and legal technologists alongside traditional lawyers. They are investing in the unglamorous plumbing of modern data infrastructure: curating proprietary corpora; building vector stores and knowledge graphs; and training domain-specific models on decades of their own work product. This is expensive, technically complex, and requires a lot of patience. However, the payoff is a genuine data moat – proprietary datasets and custom-trained models that competitors cannot easily replicate. A firm with a vast, multi-jurisdictional repository of cross-border regulatory filings can train models that understand legal nuance in ways that generic, publicly trained large language models (LLMs) simply cannot match. A firm that has systematically captured and structured decades of litigation outcomes can build predictive tools that offer quantified insights, not just qualitative opinions.

The business model implications are profound. AI creators are not just billing more efficiently for the same work. Rather, they are building new revenue streams – subscription-based legal products, continuous compliance monitoring services, and API-driven data feeds – that mirror software economics, rather than professional services economics. They are decoupling price from time, offering fixed fees for productized matter types, and introducing platform subscriptions, in which clients pay for technology access plus variable fees for incremental work.

These firms are also reshaping their workforce by hiring for skills that traditional law firms never needed: machine learning engineers to fine-tune models; product managers to define data offerings; and data architects to design client-facing APIs. They are training their lawyers not just to use AI tools, but to think in terms of data assets – to see each piece of work product as a potential training input; each clause library as a structured dataset; and each client deliverable as a machine-readable data object.

From the corporate client perspective, the distinction is stark. When a firm presents its AI strategy and the core message is "We have licensed Harvey and CoCounsel," that firm looks indistinguishable from dozens of others – and indistinguishable from us, the client, because we have licensed the same tools. When a firm shows up with a proprietary, multi-jurisdictional breach notification engine it built on its own curated corpus, reducing response times from days to minutes, that is a different conversation entirely. One is a feature announcement; the other is a competitive advantage.

The challenge for most firms is that becoming an AI creator requires investments that traditional partnership economics make nearly impossible. Partners expect their profits to be distributed annually, leaving little capital for multi-year R&D. Building proprietary AI capabilities demands patience, technical expertise, and a willingness to tolerate near-term margin pressure for long-term strategic positioning. Most firms will choose the adopter path, because it is faster, cheaper, and safer. However, from the client side, only the creators will command premium pricing and strategic relationships. The adopters will compete on price.

Some firms are already making this choice. DLA Piper built ButterflAI in-house to maintain data control. Baker McKenzie has developed proprietary legal AI capabilities across multiple jurisdictions. These firms are not just adopting technology – they are creating it. That makes all the difference in their client relationships.

The service model revolution: from transactions to data products

Understanding how these changing needs should transform law firm service offerings is where the opportunity for genuine innovation exists. It means creating a new category of service: the legal data product.

Revolutionizing legal-as-a-service subscriptions

This model fundamentally transforms legal-as-a-service (LaaS) subscriptions and self-service offerings. Today's LaaS is often a retainer for a block of lawyer hours or access to a generic hotline. The future LaaS is a data subscription: instead of buying law firm time, corporate clients buy access to law firm intelligence infrastructure. For a fixed monthly fee, corporate clients get:

- Access to law firm APIs;
- A certain number of data product updates;
- A quota of queries against custom-tuned LLMs; and
- Integrated feeds into their compliance and matter management systems.

It is predictable, scalable, and deeply integrated into corporate workflow. The law firm becomes a utility, in the best sense of the word – a reliable, always-on source of structured legal intelligence. Consider this example: a leading firm created a contract analysis API for clients. Instead of "Send us your contracts and we will review them," the offering is "Connect our API to your CLM and get real-time risk scoring as you draft." The firm generates revenue from its expertise, without requiring lawyer time on every contract.

This is not about reducing law firm fees (although efficiency gains may flow through); instead, it is about creating new revenue streams by packaging law firm expertise as continuously accessible data products, rather than discrete deliverables.

Self-service platforms: enabling client autonomy

The phrase "self-service" makes some law firms nervous, as it may sound like automating themselves out of work. However, that comes from a misunderstanding of what sophisticated clients mean by self-service. Corporate legal departments do not want self-service for complex legal advice; rather, they want self-service for the 80 percent of work that does not require law firm expert judgment, but currently necessitates law firm involvement because the infrastructure does not exist for clients to do it themselves. Self-service in an API-first world looks like:

- We can query your regulatory knowledge base programmatically;
- We can access your clause library with our own risk parameters;
- We can run contract variations through your risk assessment model; and
- We can get automated checklists and guidance for routine processes.

You remain involved in the 20 percent of work that actually requires legal judgment. Meanwhile, we handle routine items faster and cheaper, and you focus your talent on high-value work. The firms that build these platforms are not losing work – they are capturing more of our legal needs by making it frictionless to engage with them. The firms that insist we go through your associates for everything are creating friction that makes us look for alternatives.

Data products: your knowledge as inventory

Here is an unconventional thought: your historical work product is inventory that is currently sitting unused. What if you treated it as such? Examples of data products clients would pay for include:

- **Market intelligence database:** Structured data on deal terms, pricing benchmarks, and time-to-close metrics, based on your M&A practice.
- **Risk factor library:** Tagged and categorized issues from past transactions, with frequency data and resolution approaches.
- **Judicial tendency analysis:** Structured data on judges' patterns in specific case types (for litigation planning).

- **Regulatory change timeline predictions:** Based on your government affairs practice and historical data.

Notice these are not "legal advice"; they are data products derived from your expertise and experience. They are valuable because they are quantified, structured, and can feed directly into our decision systems. Some firms worry that this commoditizes their expertise. However, I would argue the opposite: it monetizes knowledge that currently generates no revenue after the matter closes. It also creates stickiness – clients who integrate your data products into their systems are much less likely to switch providers.

The KM professional's new job description

Let me address something that does not get said often enough, and that you – if you are a KM professional reading this chapter – need to understand clearly: your role is changing, and you are central to whether your firm succeeds or fails in this transformation. This book is written for you. You have probably felt this already: with the advent of generative AI (genAI), your work has moved back into the spotlight. GenAI has made foundational knowledge architecture central to legal innovation again. You are not being replaced, but your job is evolving as the firm adapts. Your new job is as much outside-in as it is inside-out. Historically, you optimized KM for the law firm's convenience; currently, your emerging role is to design knowledge as a product that your clients consume. This shift from internal optimization to external value creation is the core transformation. You remain the keeper of your firm's knowledge, but you now also understand that knowledge as a business asset, not just an operational resource.

Why you matter

Your core responsibilities – organizing knowledge, building taxonomies, maintaining precedent libraries – remain essential. However, you are now also becoming the orchestrator of the firm's internal knowledge and data infrastructure, ensuring everything is findable, structured, and AI-ready. In this new landscape, being a KM professional means building the connected, high-quality foundation on which genAI and legaltech can operate. While automation experts and legal engineers push the boundaries of delivery to clients, you enable them to do so at scale and with trust. Your expertise sits at the intersection of process, information governance, data quality, and legal know-how, making you indispensable to any firm's digital ambitions.

What this requires from you

This does not require you to become a technologist or product manager, but to understand enough about data structures, metadata, and workflow integration to collaborate with those who are. You translate legal content into structured assets; set the ground rules for capture, flow, and reuse; and ensure that, when new roles – legal engineers or tech specialists – build client-facing systems, the data backbone is robust. KM's greatest influence now is as the internal orchestrator and standards-setter – the one who designs and enforces the knowledge and data environment that all other roles (and all automation) depend on. The spotlight is back, and so is the responsibility. Legal AI may be transformative, but it is only as good as the foundations you build and maintain. That is not pressure – it is your chance to lead from where you sit.

The uncomfortable truths: strategic challenges

Some observations rarely make it into polite conversation between firms and clients, yet they illuminate the current landscape.

Data quality matters more than AI sophistication

Corporate legal departments that have built their own AI systems learn this lesson quickly: the sophistication of the model matters less than the quality and uniqueness of data. A simple model trained on clean, comprehensive, proprietary data outperforms sophisticated models trained on messy, inconsistent data. Many law firms are investing in advanced AI while neglecting the unglamorous work of data architecture: creating taxonomies, standardizing metadata, cleaning historical records, establishing governance. The corporate perspective is that we would rather work with a firm that has excellent data architecture and basic AI than cutting-edge AI with poor data quality. When corporate systems integrate with law firm systems, law firm data problems become our problems.

The billable hour paradox

The traditional law firm business model, which equates hours worked with revenue, is fundamentally at odds with the efficiency promise of AI. Every task that an AI tool automates is a potentially lost billable hour. This creates an internal disincentive to adopt technologies that streamline work, even when those technologies would deliver superior client value. How does a firm bill for an API call? How does it value a knowledge graph? This requires a radical shift from time-based to value-based pricing. It requires law firms to see their knowledge not as a byproduct of billable work to be given away for free, but as a valuable, packaged asset in its own right. The mathematics of this paradox are unforgiving: across many practice areas, roughly 30–60 percent of billable hours are devoted to repeatable, rules-based tasks – the very category of work that AI can often reduce by about 50–90 percent. For law firms, AI adoption creates an impossible choice: adopt AI and watch hours (and revenue) fall, or resist AI and watch sophisticated clients defect to more efficient competitors. One innovation leader at a top ten firm summarized it thus: "We will eat into our write-down buffer because fees are so high with how efficient we are. We need business development to be supercharged because we need to redeploy those hours or end up having to look at fixed fees."[10]

This creates what some call a "utilization crisis": when AI compresses work that previously required armies of associates, firms suddenly have too many lawyers for too little work. Without fundamental pricing transformation, AI adoption doesn't improve margins – it destroys them. This is why many firms' AI strategies remain tentative, despite public enthusiasm: the technology works, but the economics don't. The firms that crack this code first will lock in the most sophisticated clients.

The roadmap: how to get from here to there

Some observers argue that the structural challenges mentioned make incumbent transformation impossible. The reality is more nuanced: transformation is possible, but only for firms willing to fundamentally reimagine their economics along with their technology. The partnership structure, the billable hour model, and the cultural attachment to time-based value are all formidable obstacles, but they are not insurmountable. They simply require leadership who is willing to make genuinely difficult choices, rather than cosmetic changes.

From a client perspective, the path looks deceptively simple. The first step is to "make your data AI-ready": clean up taxonomies, harmonize matter types, enforce consistent templates, and deploy AI-assisted tagging and metadata extraction to kill off manual filing. The next step is to "build client-ready data feeds": expose secure APIs, define standard data schemas with pilot clients, and turn your best internal knowledge assets into structured, queryable products. The final step is to "productize and price": wrap those capabilities in clear commercial models – subscriptions, outcome-based fees, and joint R&D arrangements – that align partner economics with the efficiencies your technology actually delivers. Law firms that succeed in this transformation are not those that resist corporate demands, but which recognize this as an opportunity for genuine partnership. The best outcomes come when firms proactively embrace the questions clients are asking and collaborate on building answers together.

The transformation also requires new organizational capabilities throughout the firm. At CrowdStrike, leadership backed mandatory AI training for all legal staff to improve literacy and competence at speed. At Repsol, the legal department partnered with IE Law School and Harvard Law School to train staff worldwide in standardized methodologies.[11] Law firms need similar investments: KM professionals learning product management and data architecture; lawyers becoming comfortable with contemporaneous knowledge capture and structured documentation; and leadership developing fluency in subscription and platform business models. From the client perspective, the firms worth partnering with are those that recognize this is not about optimizing the existing model, but building something genuinely different. They treat their historical work product as a data asset to be structured and productized, not just archived. They build APIs and integration capabilities that allow bidirectional data flow between firm and client systems. They price based on outcomes and value, not inputs and time. Finally, they demonstrate willingness to share efficiency gains with clients through genuinely lower costs, not just faster delivery at the same price. The question is not whether law firms can transform, but which ones will find the leadership courage to do so before their clients force the issue.

Conclusion: become the digital partner

Let me close with this: I have not written this chapter to criticize law firms or to suggest corporate legal departments do not need them. My argument is quite the opposite: corporate legal teams need sophisticated legal partners more than ever, as the legal challenges that corporate departments face are becoming more complex. However, corporate counsel need law firms to be different kinds of partners. The regulatory environment is increasingly intricate, and business operates at speeds that seem impossible. The model where law firms hold the knowledge and clients consume advice at discrete moments is breaking down. Corporate legal departments are building the future of legal service delivery in-house on a foundation of data and AI. The model in which law firm and client data architectures integrate and jointly operate at the speed of information is the future. To achieve this, law firms must invest in unglamorous foundations: modern data infrastructure; cloud-based platforms; and robust APIs. They must develop a "Client 360" data strategy that unifies all client-related data and incorporates the client perspective. They must empower KM professionals to become product managers for legal data and train lawyers to think in terms of data assets, not just documents.

One hypothetical scenario is worth considering in this regard: if a law firm disappeared from a corporate legal department's panel tomorrow, how long would it take that department to rebuild – using other providers and internal tools – the data and AI capabilities that the firm's work currently powers inside corporate systems? If the honest answer is "not long," the firm does not yet have a data moat – it is simply another AI adopter using the same tools as the corporate legal department. The law firms that will matter most to sophisticated corporate legal departments are those whose data, models, and integrations are painful to replace.

Some law firms are already there: they have made the investments in modern data infrastructure and data literacy; built APIs and data products; and reimagined their service offerings for clients who are also AI players. They have established dedicated AI development teams that create award-winning, proprietary capabilities and launched technology ventures while retaining equity stakes. These firms do not just talk about client-centricity; rather, they have restructured their KM from the outside-in. These firms win business from sophisticated clients and command premium pricing. They are invited to strategic conversations, not just matter execution. They are positioned for a future where the provision of legal services is increasingly enabled by and delivered through technology. They have built data moats that competitors cannot easily replicate – proprietary multi-jurisdictional datasets that enable AI capabilities impossible with publicly available training data. Law firm KM professionals hold the key as to whether their firms will be leaders or followers in this transformation: they understand both the technical requirements and the business opportunity; can translate client needs into internal requirements that partners will support; and can lead the implementation of modern data infrastructure and client-facing platforms.

The question is not whether this transformation will happen; client demand makes it inevitable. The question is whether law firms will shape that future or be shaped by it. Corporate legal departments have evolved:

they have built sophisticated data architectures because their businesses demanded it, and they are now asking law firms to evolve with them. This is not to make law firm lives more difficult; instead, it is because law firm legal expertise and corporate data infrastructure working in harmony can accomplish things that neither party could achieve alone. That is the partnership that clients are seeking, and that is the client mandate for the future of legal KM. The choice belongs to law firms, but they should choose quickly, as business will not wait.

References

1 Huber N, "Four champions of the need for speed in legal operations", *Financial Times*, 5 November 2025. See: https://www.ft.com/content/66dfb8c0-cc7a-4716-b3e8-8cb9185be209.

2 *Ibid.*

3 McChrystal S, *Team of Teams: New Rules of Engagement for a Complex World*, New York: Portfolio/Penguin, 2015.

4 Huber N, "Four champions of the need for speed in legal operations", *Financial Times*, 5 November 2025. See: https://www.ft.com/content/66dfb8c0-cc7a-4716-b3e8-8cb9185be209.

5 Batraski E, "Death of the Billable Hour: Legal's $900B AI Repricing", Substack, 12 August 2025. See: https://substack.com/home/post/p-170631529.

6 *Ibid.*

7 Bucerius Law School and Simon Kucher, *The AI-Conomics of Legal Services: How generative AI will transform the commercial model of law*, 2025. See: https://www.law-school.de/fileadmin/content/law-school.de/de/units/abt_education/Studienseite/Studien/Bucerius_CLP_AI-Conomics_Studie_2025.pdf.

8 Harvey, "Harvey & Pablo Blanco Pérez (General Counsel, Repsol)", YouTube, 18 October 2025. See: https://www.youtube.com/watch?v=DtZyl6wZTqQ.

9 Lambert Y, "Companies' legal teams feel the AI spark", *Financial Times*, 19 September 2025. See: https://www.ft.com/content/e4609b0a-15f1-4256-8056-3364d991ec59.

10 Batraski E, "Death of the Billable Hour: Legal's $900B AI Repricing", Substack, 12 August 2025. See: https://substack.com/home/post/p-170631529.

11 Huber N, "Four champions of the need for speed in legal operations", *Financial Times*, 5 November 2025. See: https://www.ft.com/content/66dfb8c0-cc7a-4716-b3e8-8cb9185be209.

About Globe Law and Business

Globe Law and Business was established in 2005. From the very beginning, we set out to create legal books that are sufficiently high level to be of real use to the experienced professional, yet still accessible and easy to navigate. Most of our authors are drawn from Magic Circle and other top commercial firms, both in the United Kingdom and internationally.

Our titles are carefully produced, with the utmost attention paid to editorial, design and production processes. We hope this results in high-quality publications that are easy to read and a pleasure to own.

In 2021, we were very pleased to announce the start of a new chapter for Globe Law and Business following the acquisition of law books under the imprint Ark Publishing. Our law firm management list is now significantly expanded with many well-known and loved Ark Publishing titles.

We have also launched an online content platform, Globe Law Online, which allows for easy access across firms. Details of all titles included can be found at www.globelawonline.com. Email glo@globelawandbusiness.com for further details and to arrange a free trial for you or your firm.

We'd very much like to hear from you with your thoughts and ideas for improving what we offer. Please do feel free to email me at sian@globelawandbusiness.com. Happy reading and thank you for your time.

Sian O'Neill
Managing director
Globe Law and Business
www.globelawandbusiness.com

www.ingramcontent.com/pod-product-compliance
Ingram Content Group UK Ltd.
Pitfield, Milton Keynes, MK11 3LW, UK
UKHW060406270126
467270UK00013B/45

9 781837 231676